How did tl  Down at Ladore?

By David Beach

Table of Contents

Introduction

In southern Neosho County, Kansas, at the end of a narrow half-mile long gravel road, lies a small cemetery. I came upon the Ladore Cemetery while in the process of traveling the various backroads and side roads of Labette and Neosho counties in pursuit of my hobby of taking pictures. I would take pictures of old barns, of the animals I would encounter, the flowers and whatever else happened to catch my eye. Of particular interest was taking pictures along the feeder creeks tributary to the Neosho River and

along the Neosho River itself. There are many scenic spots along these bodies of water and many abandoned railroad and road bridges to discover as the years pass and the ways we take to get from here to there change.

Knowing that many of these back country cemeteries were attached to small towns or villages, I became curious if the Ladore Cemetery was named after the township in which it is located or if there was a town attached to the graveyard.

A search in the Chanute Library's history room brought me to W.W. Graves' two volume set on the history of Neosho County and an article in the Kansas City *Times* in 1971 on the subject of the Ladore Tragedy.

There were only a few pages written about the place, and I was curious what more was there to find. W.W. Graves was a newspaper editor located in St. Paul, Kansas, Neosho County up until his death in the early 1950's and the Neosho County Historical Society Museum in St. Paul still publishes copies of his books. So a visit to the museum in St. Paul allowed me to get copies of the books and to search through the microfilm files of the Osage Mission / Neosho County *Journal* of the 1860's and 1870's. This was the beginning of a to date three year research project on the ghost towns of Ladore and Jacksonville and the towns of Chanute and Parsons in southeast Kansas. Where before there were but few pages on Ladore, mostly on the lynching that took place there and the legends of its end; I have managed to compile and transcribe about 400 pages of material dating from the 1850's to modern day that are pertinent to the history of the little and long lost town.

The town has a colorful history and was founded by a most colorful man, James N. Roach. It produced some remarkable people and there is more to its story than its historical reputation as a sinful, wild west town would lend a person to believe. This book represents my attempt to tell Ladore's story completely, from an exploration of the history and character of the man who founded the settlement under its original name of Fort Roach to the complete history of the town before and after the lynching took place in 1870. I hope the reader enjoys reading story of the town of Ladore as much as I have enjoyed discovering and attempting to tell it.

Acknowledgements

Thanks are to be given to the various museums and libraries in southeast Kansas, each of which contributed some material for this book and each being staffed by helpful, enthusiastic people. Particular thanks goes to the Parsons Historical Society Museum, the Neosho County Historical Society Museum, the history museums in Oswego, Chetopa, and McCune, the Chanute, Parsons, Girard, Independence and Erie Public Libraries, the genealogical societies in Fort Scott, KS and Vinita, OK, and the Kansas State Historical Society.

Chapter 1: "Old Fort" / Fort Roach

Introductory Biography of James N. Roach:

Stories can start with events, or they can start with people. The story of Ladore starts with a person, a very colorful person, named James N. Roach. According to U.S. Census records and his gravestone in Vinita, OK, James Roach was born on October 22, 1818 somewhere in Virginia. At this writing and after searching census records, the exact place in Virginia is not currently known. Roach, as so many in the United States at the time, seemed to follow an urge to move west as the country expanded during the 19th Century. He next appears in the public record in Carroll County, Indiana where his marriage to his wife, Elizabeth, is recorded on September 16, 1839 **[W11. Marriage Records - Ancestry.Com]**. He was

almost 21 at the time and she was around the age of 27 or 28, having been born in Ohio sometime in 1812, and from all appearances on her third marriage, having been previously married to a man named Harness in 1832 (child John Harness), a man named William Dickinson (or Dickerson) by 1835 (child William Calvin Dickerson) and then James Roach in 1839 **[N25. *Grand Laker* – July 5, 2012 – "Pushin' Up the Daisies", by Betsy Warner – Craig County, OK, Genealogical Society]**. Elizabeth and James had children Jemima, Jeremiah, Addison, Sophia and Henrietta during the period from 1840 to 1853 **[W11. Census Records – Ancestry.Com and N25. *Grand Laker*]**. Elizabeth and James were married until her death in 1887 in Craig County, OK. They are buried in the same plot in Fairview Cemetery, Vinita, OK; James having died in February, 1895.

Despite his southern roots, James Roach was active in the Whig Party, then the Republican Party and was very strongly in the anti-slavery / free soil camp by the time he arrived in Kansas Territory in 1857 **[N16. Logansport *Democratic Pharos*, N17. Logansport *Journal*, N25. *Grand Laker*]**. The 1850 Census locates the residence of James and Elizabeth Roach in Deer Creek Township, Cass County, Indiana. An article in the Logansport (IN) *Journal* of August 4, 1852, detailing the Whig Party County Convention of that year, lists James Roach as a delegate to the congressional convention to be held later that year in Plymouth, Indiana. The Logansport *Democratic Pharos* in two issues in July, 1851, records that James N. Roach was called to be the chairman of the Deer Creek Township Tax Meeting, a meeting at which a series of resolutions were passed calling for changes in tax policy in Cass County and in the state of Indiana. The purpose of the meeting was stated in the article on July 2, 1851:

--"for the purpose of taking into consideration the propriety of petitioning the next Legislature to repeal the present unjust and unequal laws in regard to assessing and collecting taxes on Real Estate for Road and County Revenue, and pass others in their stead which will bring the burthen more equally upon the taxpaying portion of the State."

– Logansport *Democratic Pharos* – July 2, 1851

From these two initial points it can be inferred that Mr. Roach was active politically, of conservative disposition, and willing to take leadership when called upon in support of his political views. An estray notice published in the Logansport *Journal* on October 11, 1854, concerning the disposition of a lost horse and its appraised value, shows that by 1854 James Roach had sought election for and won the position of Justice of the Peace for Cass County, Indiana. This justifies a nickname often applied to Mr. Roach during his time in Kansas as "Judge" Roach, as seen in the following quotes:

--"The irrepressible Judge Roach, of Ladore, spent a few days in town this week. The Judge has always been a staunch Republican …"

- Neosho County *Journal*, January 27, 1872

--"Judge J.N. Roach, usually known in these parts by the endearing name "Old Fort," has been in the city during the week attending to legal business."

– Neosho County *Journal*, December 9, 1871

The two previous quotes illustrate that the "Judge" nickname stuck long after his time in Indiana.

The level of political activity, leadership and depth of his feelings towards the issues that were building up in the country over the slavery question and in Kansas Territory in particular is illustrated with several passages from the Logansport *Democratic Pharos* of July 23, 1856, detailing the particulars of the Jackson Township Democratic Meeting. The following excerpts from that article are pertinent here:

--"On motion, the following persons were appointed a committee to report the names of officers for the Club: Phillip D. Kemp, Isaac Goldsberry, David Fickle, Jno. Roach, Wm. Frush.

Dr. Adrain then addressed the meeting in a happy manner for more than an hour and a half, showing up the workings and fruits of the "Emigrant Aid Societies" and "Border Ruffians" – the beauties and consistencies of the Know Nothings and self-styled Republicans – and who were responsible for the present state of things in Kansas.

S.A. Hall followed in a speech abounding in facts and arguments."

- Logansport *Democratic Pharos*, July 23, 1856

The meeting took part over two days, and adjourned at the close of the first day after the events described in the above quoted passage. The follow-up occurred when the meeting re-convened the following morning.

--"By resolution of the Club, James N. Roach then took the floor, and labored for an hour and a half in a vain attempt to refute the positions and arguments of Messrs. Adrain and Hall.

It was upon the head of S.A. Hall that the vials of his wrath were poured out. Said he had taken notes during the afternoon on purpose to be used in demolishing Mr. Hall; and that he (Roach) had a pile of documents to prove that Hall uttered falsehoods, and that the Democrats were in favor of extending slavery."

- Logansport *Democratic Pharos*, July 23, 1856

The author of the article in the *Pharos* described Mr. Roach's performance at the meeting as follows: "He worried himself nearly out in heaping vilifications and abuse on Mr. Hall and the Democratic Party."

The "over the top" nature of his personality will be seen later during his time in Kansas. That Mr. Roach was attending and recognized at a Democratic Party meeting either says something as to his status as a public figure in that area at the time, or that perhaps he had spent some time in the Democratic Party after the collapse of the Whig Party and before the Republican Party which followed it had fully gained back power and influence. That the events in Kansas Territory at that time were of concern to Mr.

Roach are indicated by his performance at that meeting in July, 1856, and by the fact that, as nearly as can be ascertained, he and his family had moved to Bourbon County, Kansas sometime in 1857.

Fort Roach in Fort Scott:

James Roach and family moved to Bourbon County, Kansas sometime in 1857, near the site of the federal facility, Fort Scott (the town itself not yet having been established). He is mentioned several times by the Fort Scott *Monitor* in the 1870's after his leaving Bourbon County for Neosho County, Kansas and appears in several articles published in the *Monitor* that provide details as to the founding and early history of the town of Fort Scott that were published during the first two decades of the 20th century. There are several passages in Charles Goodlander's memoirs of the founding of Fort Scott and in articles published in the Fort Scott *Monitor* that shed further light on Mr. Roach's political leanings and also help fill in some points as to later events in Ft. Roach/Ladore, Kansas; the town Mr. Roach helped found in Neosho County.

In the July 21, 1910 issue of the *Monitor*, the paper interviewed a pioneer settler of Fort Scott named Ben Files as to the early days of that city. The title of the article is **"A Bandit Used to Own Fort Scott. He Sold to the Town Company."** In the article are the details supplied by Mr. Files as to the acquisition of the property by the Fort Scott Town Company.

--**"The 160 acres upon which the town of Fort Scott stands was originally the property of a man named Roach, who was familiarly known as Fort Roach."**

--**"He preempted the 160 acres from the government and held it, expecting to make a big wad of money out of it someday. But he didn't. One day the original town company was formed and they went to Roach and made him sell forty acres of his 160 to them. Under threat that he** would be hung, he yielded, says Mr. Files. He afterwards sold the remainder of the 160 and got out of the country."

Mr. Files also made the following statements as to Mr. Roach in the same article:

--"Mr. Files says he was a bandit who had committed many crimes in Southwestern Missouri and Kansas."

--"He says he was one of John Brown's men who got down here and commenced a reign of terror."

--"'I will never forget one incident that happened along in those days,' says Mr. Files. 'I was down in Barton County, Mo., and Roach came up to me and said he would give me $25 in gold if I would drive him to Fort Scott. In those days $25 in gold was worth $150 as compared with the present time. I didn't know the road very well, but I got one of my men to bring him to Fort Scott. I learned afterwards that he had been lower down in the country and had committed some robbery and that a posse was after him.'"

- Fort Scott *Monitor*, July 21, 1910, "A Bandit Used to Own Fort Scott"

Mr. Files also mentioned that the posse had at one point captured Mr. Roach and tried to hang him.

In an article in the *Grand Laker* newspaper, published in Oklahoma, Betsy Warner of the Craig County Genealogical Society published this passage in 2012 as to James Roach's days in Fort Scott.

--"Roach's home in Ft. Scott was often called "Fort Roach" and a popular meeting spot for abolitionist John Brown and his fellow Jayhawkers."

- The *Grand Laker*, July 5, 2012

--"At first the family lived in Fort Scott; where Roach was involved in the Jayhawkers movement and entertained John Brown and the abolitionists."

- The *Grand Laker*, July 12, 2012

That Mr. Roach would be a supporter and perhaps even cohort of John Brown in Kansas is not surprising, considering the published political views he espoused while in Indiana. If he was in fact an ally of John Brown and had "commenced a reign of terror" while in Kansas it makes there being a posse after him while he was fleeing Barton County in southwest Missouri understandable. During the "Bleeding Kansas" days, there were many groups on both sides of the Kansas – Missouri border taking advantage of a relatively lawless situation to spread terror and rob and pillage in the name of having Kansas enter the Union as either a free or slave state. As Mr. Roach lived openly in Kansas and was never quiet as to his political leanings and felt secure enough in his public life to at one point run for the Kansas Legislature, it seems to indicate he felt comfortable as to his actions in his early days in Kansas and their subsequent public perception.

Charles W. Goodlander, in his memoirs of early Fort Scott, had these passages in his book as to James N. "Old Fort" Roach.

--"On the corner of National Avenue and First Street, where the feed store now is, was what was called Fort Roach, occupied by Roach and his family."

--"The politics of the inhabitants at that time was border ruffian, pro-slavery democrats and free-state democrats. There were only two republicans – Tom Roberts and Old Roach. The free-state and pro-slavery democrats were about equal in number."

--"At this time all the citizens of Fort Scott were either pro-slavery or free state democrats, except Tom Roberts and Old Roach, who being the only republicans, naturally were quite intimate."

-"Memoirs and Recollections of C.W. Goodlander"; Fort Scott Monitor Press, 1900

So, it seems reasonably clear that Mr. Roach emigrated from Indiana to Kansas in the late 1850's in support of the free-state movement and principles and against the pro-slavery movement in Kansas Territory. It also appears that Mr. Roach shared both the convictions and willingness to act, perhaps even beyond the law, in support of his beliefs that John Brown exhibited. The degree to which Mr. Roach was actually associated with John Brown is still not clear. Mr. Roach in one sense was a founder of Fort Scott, at least so far as the fact that the town was founded on what had originally been his land. Based upon census records and Goodlander's memoirs, Mr. Roach ran a boarding house / saloon in Fort Scott at the northwest corner of National Avenue and First Street. Mr. Roach was also referred to as "Fort" Roach or "Old Fort" based on the naming of his place in Fort Scott.

As a further description or depiction of the character of that life in Fort Scott at "Fort" Roach, Mr. Goodlander had this to say in his memoirs.

--"Fort Roach, as we used to call the house the Roach family lived in, was a resort for the boys where they danced on the puncheon floor. Roach and his family were from Posey County, Indiana, and the music at the dance was usually to the tune of "Hell on the Wabash." Sometimes these dances would last all night and all the next day. I have known of one dance that lasted two nights and one day."

-"Memoirs and Recollections of C.W. Goodlander"; Fort Scott Monitor Press, 1900

Mr. Goodlander also mentions a story told by one George Clark of a "bear parade" complete with band, that some of the boys of Fort Scott once undertook to create, using a pet bear that Mr. Roach used to keep on a chain at his home. The parade apparently ended when the bear finally got annoyed and bit one of the participants. It must be noted that the above quoted passage is of some importance in adding detail and some explanation as to the events in May, 1870 in Ladore, Neosho County, Kansas, commonly known as the "Ladore Tragedy" that took place at Mr. Roach's boarding house in that community. Some comments about the town of Ladore and about the events of that night in May are more comprehensible in view of the comments of life at the Roach house in Fort Scott.

As near as can be determined, James Roach and his family left Fort Scott and Bourbon County sometime in either 1867 or 1868, moving down near the southern boundary of Neosho County, Kansas. There he founded a settlement along the banks of Labette Creek in Ladore Township. Based upon currently known sources, the reasons for the move are not completely clear. In Mr. Files' recollections in the 1910 article in the *Monitor*, he gives the impression that Mr. Roach was more or less forced to sell part of his property for the town site, and perhaps more or less forced at a later time to sell the rest of it and leave Fort Scott. However, comments made in reference to James Roach in articles in the *Monitor* in the 1870's are generally appreciative and respectful of the man. In an article published in the *Monitor* on February 2, 1870, a correspondent for the paper, touring southern Neosho County and profiling the new towns and people in that locality, made this comment as the Union Pacific, Southern Branch (soon to be the Missouri, Kansas & Texas) railroad was building down towards Ft. Roach/Ladore through Neosho County:

--"Captain Ayers, who returned from Ladore yesterday, informed me that 400 laborers have arrived at that place, to work on the Southern Branch Road. They were waiting for the engineers, who were behind with their work, but grading will commence in a day or two. Ladore (late Fort Roach), is to be a point on the road. Our old friend and former fellow townsman, J. N. Roach, will thus become a fortunate man, and if he plays his cards judiciously he may soon be one of the solid men of Neosho County. Roach always had an eye for business, and it may be that he knew all the time that a railroad would hunt him out."

- Fort Scott *Monitor*, February 2, 1870

Based on this passage "our old friend and fellow townsman" Roach was, at least for the *Monitor*, not someone who was forced from the town. In the opinion of the correspondent, one reason for Roach's move may have been in order to locate along the line of a newly built railroad on land to be had cheaply and take advantage of the coming prosperity the road would bring.

Potentially another reason for the move to Neosho County was a murder that occurred in Fort Scott, perhaps at Fort Roach, which involved Mr. Roach's son-in-law Major John David Mefford and a man named Thomas Dilworth, which occurred in October, 1867. A short article on this affair was published in the Kansas *Daily Tribune*, published in Lawrence, Kansas, on October 23rd of that year.

--"SHERIFF HARRIS, of Fort Scott, passed through our city yesterday, having in charge Major Mefford, who killed Thomas Dilworth, and was sentenced to the Penitentiary for ten years. He was major of the Sixth Kansas, and was generally spoken of as a good soldier, but addicted to drunken sprees. Our readers will recollect that this murder occurred at a Republican meeting the night before the last election. Mefford was intoxicated, and commenced a disturbance when Dilworth remonstrated and stopped him. Mefford met Dilworth a short time after and shot him."

- Kansas *Daily Tribune* (Lawrence), October 23, 1867

Nothing has been found to date in print in relation to Mr. Roach that would directly connect this event with his relocation to Neosho County. However, it would have been not long after this event that apparently the decision was made by Roach to move from Fort Scott to Neosho County. In either case, the earliest mentions of the settlement of Fort Roach appear in the Neosho County newspapers in 1868, detailing a time when there were but one or two houses on the site during the spring of that year.

James Roach would reside in Kansas for nine years after establishing the settlement in Neosho County. He and his family would leave the Ladore area and move to Craig County, Oklahoma while it was still the Indian Territory and reside there for the rest of his life. This narrative will return to Mr. Roach after exploring the history and legacy of the town he helped to found.

Chapter 2: Early Days in Ladore Township

The brief mentions of Ladore that can be found in the history books mainly concern themselves with the events of May, 1870, known as the Ladore Tragedy or Ladore Lynching. If not for the saga of the "Bloody Benders" in 1873, the crime claim to fame for Neosho County and Labette County Kansas would have been written on a single bloody night in the spring of 1870. The Ladore Tragedy will be explored in great detail later in this book, but the goal of this work is also to give a telling of the events and development of Fort Roach / Ladore both in the years before the lynching took place and afterwards, when the opening of the Osage Ceded Lands to railroad companies helped bring about Ladore's end as an incorporated city and turn it into a lost town of Kansas.

1868-69

Correspondents

What is known of many of the towns in the early days of Kansas comes from the writings of editors and columnists in the local papers. Many people would live in a particular town and write a weekly or bi-weekly column for nearby papers as an unofficial correspondent for that paper. Fort Roach / Ladore never had its own paper, but it did have an attraction, probably because of the construction of the Leavenworth, Lawrence & Galveston (L.L.&G.) and the Missouri, Kansas & Texas (M.K.&T.) railroads through Neosho County and the location of the town site relative to the M.K.&T., for correspondents from papers in Kansas.

During the time prior to the arrival of the M.K.&T. in Ladore, the town had two local correspondents writing for different papers in

Kansas. The first wrote under the name of "Ex-Typo," and in his writings for the Osage Mission *Journal* from 1868-69 documented the development of Ladore from the time when there were but two or three buildings on the site to the plans to build its first schoolhouse. "Ex-Typo" was later identified as a man named Lewis (or Louis) Reese, who was active in Democratic Party politics in the area. The other "local" correspondent wrote under the name Wheeler for the Lawrence *Daily Republican Journal* during the year 1870. It is unclear if Wheeler was using a pseudonym or not. Later articles mention a family by name of Wheeler residing in Ladore Township, and Wheeler wrote as a resident of the area, so it is possible that the real name of the author was used.

In addition to the local correspondents, papers from northern areas in Kansas would periodically send reporters through the area of southeastern Kansas to travel on the railroad lines being constructed, or on the roads if there were no railroads, in order to write profiles of the area and of the towns that were being founded and developed in the region. The Fort Scott *Monitor* and other papers would often send correspondents through the area. For towns such as Ladore with no local paper on site, it is to these sources that a debt is owed as to information of the early conditions on site.

Ex-Typo, writing a column generally titled in some version of "Fort Roach Eye-Teams" gave much good detail in several columns as to the development of the settlement of Fort Roach / Ladore. In a column for the Osage Mission *Journal* in December of 1868, Reese identifies Byron P. Ayres as the secretary of the Town Company and mentions that in the spring of '68 there were but two buildings on the town site, but that by December there were, by count, "thirty seven houses either built or in process of erection." Official records found in Kansas State Historical Society microfilms show the

Kinman Town Company as being incorporated in July of 1869, so this mention of a town company predates the official record by about a year. The Kinman Co. was changed to the Ladore Town Company later in 1869. He mentions that the main state road from Humboldt to Oswego ran through the town site (the M.K.&T. later paralleling this route when constructing the rail line through Neosho County). He mentions that most of the incoming settlers were, based on his observation "of that energetic, progressive style who make respectable and permanent citizens." This comment is important to note in light of Ladore's reputation as a wild, end of track western town. In addition to Roach, he notes settlers with the last names of Johnson, Ayres, Marston, Ulmer, Beard and Lamb as active on the town site. Among the buildings being built or planned he mentions a store on the southeast corner of the square, the plans to build a schoolhouse (for which James Roach donated $50) which would also double as a church, and the desire of the citizens for additional houses, churches and a lyceum [N8. **Osage Mission *Journal* December 3, 1868, January 7, 1869**].

The site of Ladore, as platted, lies between Meade and Lyon Roads in southern Neosho County in Ladore Township. The southern boundary is designated as 20th Road, placing it two miles north of the county line. The site was to occupy the two quarter sections of the section bounded by 20th and 30th roads north to south and Lyon and Meade Roads from west to east. The Ladore cemetery lies at the end of 25th road, a half mile road that would have ended at the end of Oak Street as shown on the map. The Ladore school house is indicated on old maps as being located at the northeast corner of the site along Meade Road. The plat map indicates the presence of the M.K.&T. railroad line and depot, so the official map was not platted until 1870 or after.

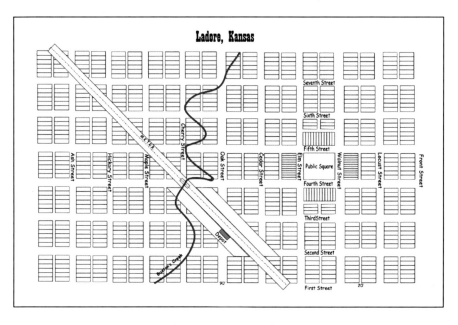

The Ladore Town Site:

This map of the Ladore site has been recreated from the plat map filed and on record at the Register of Deeds Office at the Neosho County Courthouse in Erie, KS.

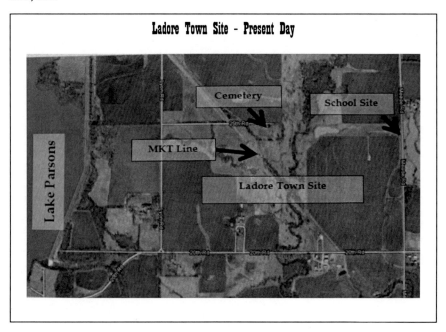

The current condition of the Ladore town site is that of farmers' fields. With reference to the graphic on the previous page, the old road bed of the M.K.&T. line is still visible as it bisects the town site diagonally. The rails were removed from this line during the mid-1980s. The school is long gone, but the cemetery is still in place and in use by residents of the area.

For reference, consultation with the Neosho County Register of Deeds Office places the original settlement and the land owned by James and Addison Roach across 20th road to the south, the Roach family owning at various times the two quarter sections south of the town site. Lewis Reese, writing from his self-named residence "Mount Dianthus" owned land just northwest of the town site.

To continue the summary of the Ex-Typo columns, at various times Reese would comment on the coming battle with the L.L.&G. and M.K.&T. railroads over settlers' rights to land in the Osage Ceded Lands (principally Neosho and Labette Counties), and would talk about developments on the town site itself, whether to fence or not fence farmer's fields and taxation issues associated with the fencing issue. The last "Ex-Typo" column found appeared in the Osage Mission *Journal* in early 1869. Reese had written the column as if others were to follow, but the reason for the end of the columns is not known.

Other news items on events and developments in Ladore were published through the year of 1869. The Kansas *Daily Tribune*, published in Lawrence, KS, published a notice in July of that year that James Roach had been had been appointed postmaster of Ladore. In the same month the Osage Mission *Journal* published an article titled "A Trip to the Verdigris" wherein their reporter was traveling across Neosho and into Montgomery County, profiling the towns and people along his route. This article mentions the store of Capt. [M.M.] Neely and business partner Adam Smith operating in Ladore. It also mentions a store being run by Squire [John] Hall being operated at the corner of Broadway and Roach Avenue. A quick look at the plat map shows no streets of those names. Evidently there were changes and perhaps a previous map that has been lost to history. It should be noted in a column later in the year mention is made that the "Kinman Town Company" had been changed to the "Ladore Town Company" and there was a man named Kinman mentioned in residence in other articles. The record seems to indicate that the plat map filed in Erie was filed by the M.K.&T. Also in the *Journal* article "A Trip to the Verdigris" the reporter reveals the identity of Lewis Reese as "Ex-Typo" indirectly by noting his home on "Mount Dianthus," a self-reference that "Ex-Typo" had made to his home in an earlier article. Whether the revelation of his pen-name was the precipitating event for the end of the "Eye-Teams" columns is not known [N8. **Osage Mission** *Journal*, **July 29, 1869; N22. Kansas** *Tribune*, **July 15, 1869]**.

One activity that seemed to occupy a lot of the political time of the newly organizing counties in southeastern Kansas seemed to be contests between the leading towns for the county seat. Neosho County was no exception to this, and probably as prolonged in the controversy of final establishment of the county seat as any. The county offices were first organized in 1864 at a meeting at a small town called Osage City, which was located on the Neosho River just northeast of the current city of Chanute. Chanute residents will know the site as the area east of the river at the site of Brown Wells dam. A concurrent name for the place was Roger's Mill. Later, in 1866, there was another organizational meeting held near Trotter's Ford at the base of the Island, at or near the site where Jacksonville, Kansas was established in Lincoln Township, at about the same time Ladore was established in 1868. The Island refers to the region southeast of Osage Mission (now St. Paul) where the Neosho River splits into two channels for several miles, rejoining at the southern point where Trotter's Ford was located. At this meeting the delegates from the southern part of the county decided to appeal to the Kansas Legislature to split Neosho County in half, establishing the new county of Labette County. The legislature did so in 1867 [B4. W.W. Graves, *History of Neosho County*].

Ladore's role in the question of determining the county seat for Neosho County was peripheral, due to its location so far south of the geographical center of the county. The main competitors for the honor were Erie and Osage Mission. Elections for county seat were called practically every year from 1868 through 1874, when the question was finally decided in the Kansas Supreme Court in favor of Erie. Each town would solicit allies in the other towns in the county. Men from Erie provided backing for the establishment of the Neosho Valley *Eagle* newspaper in Jacksonville, at the southeast corner of the county. The publisher/editor of the *Eagle* reciprocated by publicly backing Erie for county seat in its editorials [B4. Graves]. By 1869 the paper had shifted operations to Erie. In 1868 a contested election was held, first declared won by Erie, and then on subsequent recount declared won by Osage Mission. During this time the county records were clandestinely removed from Erie to Osage Mission. An article appearing in November, 1869, in the Osage Mission *Journal* details a committee meeting in Ladore, wherein the citizens of Ladore, as voiced by the committee, called for an end to further county seat elections, thus in effect declaring support for Osage Mission. This is not surprising considering the men who were operating businesses in both towns. Dr. G.W. Gabriel operated offices in both towns and served as secretary of the Ladore Town Company. Capt. M.M. Neely and brother, Dr. A.F. Neely, operated stores in both places. Dr. J.B. Lamb of Osage Mission also owned a store in Ladore. Thomas C. Cory, the first county attorney for Neosho County was an early citizen and trustee of Osage Mission who shifted his base of operations to Ladore. As named in the *Journal* article, the committee formed in Ladore to call for the end to further county seat elections consisted of Capt. Neely, Lewis Reese, Edward Maher and D.S. Beard [**N8. Osage Mission *Journal*, November 12, 1869**].

To further illustrate the influence of the Osage Mission faction in Ladore, notices published in the *Journal* later in November and December of 1869 formalized the change of the town company name from "Kinman" to "Ladore" at a stockholders meeting on the 9th of October of 1869, Kinman having first been incorporated in July of 1869 [**N27. Kansas Historical Society, Microfilm 1167 – Lost Towns of Kansas, N8. Osage Mission *Journal*, November 18, 1869**]. A notice posted in the same edition of the paper identified Dr. Gabriel as town company secretary and John Moffitt of Osage Mission as the company's general agent. The notice was posted by J. O'Grady as president of the company, who also happened to be the mayor of Osage Mission at the time, as identified in a Fort Scott *Monitor* article published in January, 1870. The original incorporators of the Kinman Town Company were D.R. Kinman, R.D. Cogswell, John O'Grady, A.F. Neely, and John Ryan.

The year of 1869 was a year of development and growth for Ladore. Businesses were opening, houses and buildings were being built, plans for schools and churches were being made and the town was beginning to find a voice in the politics of the county. The town was located on a major road running north to south through the county and it was fairly certain there would be a railroad built along that line, probably through Ladore itself. At this point the wild Ladore of infamy was not apparent, at least not any more than any other town at a similar point in its development in southeastern Kansas at that time. As the M.K.&T. built its road southward through Neosho County, this would all change.

1870 – January to May

The year 1870 would be "the" year for Ladore in so many ways. As the path of the M.K.&T. railroad construction became more publicly certain, settlers, and not all of them the desirable kind, began to move in and the development of the town accelerated. Ladore's reputation as the wild, western town was made in 1870 as the M.K.&T. built down toward and through the town.

Lewis Reese and others in the region had been warning of the upcoming controversy involving the land grants given to the L.L.&G. and M.K.&T. railroads and how these interacted with the Osage Treaty of 1865 (the Canville Treaty) which had opened Neosho and Labette counties to settlement and created the Osage Ceded Lands from the Osage Reservation. Various actions had been taken to address the problem of competing and pre-existing settlers' claims to the land prior to the land grants to the companies, including a failed and unfair and aborted treaty in 1868 (the Sturgis Treaty) and a joint resolution of Congress in 1869. Nothing had worked and both settlers and railroad companies had competing claims to what amounted to the greater proportion of the land in both counties. The future settlement and development of both counties depended upon the legal settlement of the question, and Ladore, due partly to its location in the geometric center of the ceded lands and its probable location along the line of the railroad, in 1870 would assume a major and prominent political role during that year. A thinking man at the beginning of 1870 would not have been considered wrong to consider Ladore to be the most likely place to become a major city in Neosho County based on these factors. By the end of 1870 there was probably no more famous (or infamous) town in Kansas known to the nation than Ladore, but at the same moment in history, its bubble would burst and Ladore would largely be gone before another year had passed.

Papers formed in the existing and newly formed towns on the Osage Ceded Lands would follow the progress of the M.K.&T. and L.L.&G. railroads through the region. As Ladore was located on the proposed line of the M.K.&T., the papers would document the progress of the road towards the town. The Fort Scott *Monitor* of February 2, 1870, in a profile of Osage Mission and Ladore, made the following note as to the progress of the railroad construction.

--"Captain Ayers, who returned from Ladore yesterday, informed me that 400 laborers have arrived at that place, to work on the Southern Branch Road. They were waiting for the engineers, who were behind with their work, but grading will commence in a day or two."

- Fort Scott *Monitor*, February 2, 1870 – "From Osage Mission"

The phrase "Southern Branch Road" refers to the earlier name of the M.K.&T. as the Union Pacific – Southern Branch railroad. At various times it was also referred to as the Neosho Valley road in articles. The line being built through Ladore started in Junction City and was built down through Emporia, Neosho Falls, Humboldt, the newly formed towns of Tioga and New Chicago (later merged to become Chanute), Austin, Urbana, Galesburg and Ladore and would become known as the Junction City or Neosho division of the company.

The *Monitor* article points out the influx of additional people just for railroad construction alone that was coming into Ladore. This influx of people so quickly would distort the development of any town, making demands upon goods and services that would have to be met in a quicker than expected fashion. The effect on Ladore ultimately was devastating socially while profitable economically for a time.

The second local correspondent, Wheeler, made his appearance in the Lawrence *Republican Journal* and *Western Home Journal* in

1870, starting with an article on February 10, 1870. In this first article he notes the progress of the "Southern Branch Railroad" or "Neosho Valley" road, notes the discovery of a coal vein near the town, profiles the town and what businesses are present at that point in time, and discusses the problem of claim jumping. Highlights from this article include.

--"Parties of engineers in the employ of the Southern Branch Railroad have recently been passing and repassing through the embryo city of Ladore, and have now passed on, leaving the great route ready to pass into the hands of the grading contractors."

--"The very stakes along the line of the coming railroad, pipe out a merry song of a 'good time coming;'"

--"Everbody rejoices, and young Ladore, the little city with a big future, is 'chock' full of glee."

--"A coal-bed four feet in thickness, and but about four feet beneath the surface, has recently been discovered nearly two miles west of town."

--"There are already three good drygoods and general merchandise houses in town, one butcher shop and meat market, a boot and shoe maker, a blacksmith, plow and wagon shop, a stove and hardware store, two good doctors, and the second best school house in the county."

--"Capital can here find profitable investment in almost every department of enterprise."

--"Everybody wants to get near Ladore, and claim jumping has become a perfect mania; in fact, the business is a raging epidemic throughout the Osage Lands."

- Lawrence *Western Home Journal*, February 10, 1870 - "Letter from Neosho County"

The Wheeler column is a fairly long one, as there is much to tell the reader and it does give a preview of several items that would affect the people of the Osage Ceded Lands and southeast Kansas in the succeeding years. The discovery of coal is worth remark as in the not too distant future there would be much mining done southeast Kansas, as well as strikes of oil and natural gas. The remark about claim jumping is also worth noting as within a year would be formed the Settlers' Protective Association (S.P.A.) one activity of which would be the at least semi-vigilante if not outright vigilante adjudication of claim disputes between settlers trying to homestead and pay government price for land in the area and settlers who were trying to buy their claims from the railroad land grants. This point is also pertinent to the history of Ladore as the meetings which would lead to the formation of the S.P.A. would be held in Ladore in the year 1870. The column gives a good accounting as to the business activity and improvements taking place at Ladore, and it further mentions the needs for a good hotel and industries like mills. Such columns written about and for towns and cities at that time were also part advertisement and cheer-leading activity for them. Each town was supposedly the best, had the best opportunities for growth, was located in the best geographical area and was "can't miss" for capital investors. In the case of Ladore, at least until the end of 1870, this seemed to be a general consensus among the papers of the area. Each one would remark on the railroad opportunity that would apparently be afforded to the place as the M.K.&T. built its Neosho Division down from Junction City and its Sedalia Division down from Sedalia, MO and through Fort Scott. The two divisions would intersect somewhere in southern Neosho County or northern Labette County, and many felt Ladore would be the place.

The growth and apparent future of the town of Ladore can be followed by reading through the announcements and columns published in the southeast Kansas newspapers during the late winter and early spring of 1870.

--"We learn that Fort Roach is progressing finely and that new buildings are going up as fast as ever. No less than thirty homes have been put up within the last two weeks."

- Osage Mission Journal, February 17, 1870

--"We have been reliably informed that the S.B.U.P. R.R. [Southern Branch, Union Pacific R.R.] will make Ladore a station on their road, so the timid need not fear that the cars will go buzzing through that place without making a stop. The future of Ladore is bright."

- Osage Mission Journal, March 5, 1870 – "Station at Ladore"

From these notices can be seen how the pace of construction and development of Ladore was accelerating. From the "Eye-Teams" columns, Lewis Reese makes note of the increase of buildings in Ladore over the better part of a year from two buildings to thirty seven. In the *Journal* notice of February 17, thirty buildings had gone up in less than a month. With that information and the statement about there definitely being a station built at Ladore, the information, if accurate, certainly shows an influx of people and a belief that Ladore was to be made an important point on the M.K.&T. line. As there were no other settlements then in existence with miles along the routes under construction, it was a logical belief that the junction between the M.K.&T. divisions would be made at Ladore.

Wheeler is heard from again in a letter to the Lawrence *Republican Journal* dated February 25, and published on March 8, 1870. He again advertises for the future of Ladore, makes some points about what was publicly believed about the course of railroad construction through Neosho County, and gives some observations about Fort Roach and James Roach. Some highlights from the letter include.

--"especially does young Ladore, the little city with the big future, shout for joy. The irrepressible R.S. Stevens is in town tonight, and says the cars will be running through here by the first of May."

--"It is reported, but with how much truth deponent saith not, that the Galveston will cross the Valley Road at this point."

--"I am not a member of the town company, do not even reside in town – town site on railroad land; and I hope the railroad company will take the infant city under charge, and in fostering care."

--"Fort Roach is a double-log fortification just south of Ladore. It wants no guns of heavy caliber, and is commanded, except in times of mutiny, by Gen. Roach, *alias* Fort Roach, whom the Wasaches [Osages] irreverently call 'Old Whisky Roach.'"

--"For the last fortnight Major H.C. Whitney has been going up and down Neosho and Labette counties endeavoring to stir the settlers on railroad lands up to the attempt to wrest the odd sections from the avaricious clutches of railroad monopolists."

- Lawrence *Republican Journal*, March 8, 1870 – "Letter from Neosho County"

Again in his columns and comments does Wheeler give much good information and clarification on later events at Ladore. Of debate in later years is the question of whether Ladore sealed its own fate with unrealistic land dealings with the M.K.&T. or did the railroad manipulate the situation by falsely advertising Ladore as the junction point? That discussion will take place later in this book, but two items in Wheeler's letter will be placed into evidence: the first being Robert S. Stevens, the M.K.&T. general manager, being in Ladore in early 1870 having discussions and making statements about the M.K.&T.'s role in Ladore; the second being Wheeler's statement about the "town site on railroad land." There is tax sale evidence later on that supports that statement. So a point of fact to keep in mind is that the railroad company apparently *owned* the platted town site of Ladore.

The comment Wheeler makes as to the crossing of the Galveston with the Valley Road at Ladore is worth remark as well. The crossing did take place between the Galveston (L.L.&G.) and the Valley Road (M.K.&T.) in Neosho County, but it took place in the northwest corner of the county in the summer of 1870, forming at its junction two competing towns; Tioga on the L.L.&G. side and New Chicago on the M.K.&T. side. After two years of fruitless bickering and competition, the two towns merged to form the city of Chanute.

The comment on Fort Roach and James Roach is also valuable to add detail and support to other statements to be considered later. The layout of Fort Roach is described in accounts of the Ladore Tragedy as a two story double log cabin in two separate accounts of the events of that tragic night. This statement further adds to the accuracy of the later descriptions. In addition, there are later comments as to the availability of whisky in Ladore in general and at Fort Roach in particular. This statement of Wheeler as to the Osage nickname of Roach as "Old Whisky", coupled with statements as to the dances and parties held at Fort Roach in Fort Scott in C.W. Goodlander's memoirs of early Fort Scott, seem to connect and point out that James Roach lived in Neosho County in much the same way he lived in Bourbon County. As will be noted in the recounting of the Ladore Tragedy, there are comments in people's memories as to the riotous and drunkenness that took place at Fort Roach at the time.

In Wheeler's account of the activities of Major Whitney in discussing and meeting about settlers' rights versus the railroad land grant claims, Wheeler is rather disparaging in the letter; noting that Whitney spoke in Ladore to a "slim audience" which had dropped to less than a dozen by the end of the talk. By the middle of the year of 1870 such talks and meetings would draw hundreds, if not thousands of participants. By the years 1873-74 meetings were being held claiming attendances of 7,000 in Thayer, 5,000 in Osage Mission and 10,000 persons in Parsons. Ladore would have the honor or starting the S.P.A. pebble rolling down the hill, Parsons would have the honor of collecting the reward of that effort as well.

Several notices in the papers trace the development of Ladore in the days before the arrival of the M.K.&T. line to the town in May of 1870. Some point to the positive side of the building up of a town, and part to the downsides of being an "end of the track" town in the western United States in the attraction of drinking, gambling and prostitution to the crews of the railroad workers.

--"The enterprising citizens of Ladore have issued Bonds, and are building a first class school house, 18x24 feet in size. When finished, it will be the best school house in the county, except the one in Osage Mission, which is hard to beat in point of finish."

- Osage Mission *Journal*, April 6, 1870

--"The citizens of Fort Roach have given forty acres of land near the town and subscribed $2,000 for building a Catholic church."

- Fort Scott *Monitor*, April 7, 1870

--"We learn from Dr. Gabriel that a serious fight took place on the streets of the above named town, on Sunday night last. About a dozen men engaged in the affray. Stones, clubs and pistols were freely used, and one of the combatants was shot in the neck with a pistol ball, causing a slight wound."

- Osage Mission *Journal*, April 12, 1870 – "Trouble at Fort Roach"

--"On Tuesday evening of this week, another fight occurred in the same place. A stranger was "taken in" by the "shoulder strikers." He became noisy and wanted to fight. He was accommodated, and the next day he was found with his head pounded to a jelly, and one of his legs broken. His wounds were attended to by Dr. Neely."

- Osage Mission *Journal*, April 12, 1870 – "Trouble at Fort Roach"

--"The M. K. & T. Railroad will reach Fort Roach in about fifteen days."

- Fort Scott *Monitor*, April 20, 1870

These items point to the dual track upon which Ladore was developing. On one side the town was developing rather positively as people moved in, built businesses, built homes and sought to provide the community with social strength through such things as churches and schools. On the other side, fights among "dozens of men" were becoming more common as the drinks were becoming more plentiful and the railroad was building closer and closer. Dr. George W. Gabriel, later six times elected mayor of Parsons, wrote in a memoir about his days in Ladore in the Parsons *Sun* in 1920:

--"I think there were perhaps 1,500 people living there; and there was more pure and undefiled meanness there than any other place for the size of it. You could look up the street at almost any time of the day or night and see from one to half a dozen fights going on. I had ridden down the streets more than once and seen fellows being robbed in the full light of day, almost every house had a saloon in it and those that did not had plenty to drink on the side."

– Dr. George W. Gabriel, Parsons *Sun*, March 19, 1920

In another "Letter from Neosho County" written just after the Ladore Tragedy on May 11, 1870, but not published until after the events occurred, Wheeler stated:

--"The cars will reach our young but rapidly growing city in a few days. Already the whistle of the construction train can be heard. Railroads are said to be the great civilizers of the age. In one sense, this is true; but all manner of vice and uncivilization is preceding our road. Dramshops, the very sinkholes of perdition, have multiplied, and drunken rowdies have become so bold that decent people are almost afraid to show their faces on the streets."

--"Sunday traffic was becoming quite common, until the God fearing and law abiding portion of the community met together, organized, and took steps toward putting the town on a more moral and civilized basis."

--"Today a regular old-fashioned California vigilance committee, composed of a majority of the citizens of Ladore and vicinity, took the reins in their own hands, and are running things to suit their notions of propriety and justice."

- Lawrence *Republican Journal*, May 20, 1870 – "Letter from Neosho County"

From these observations and others to be noted later, it can be seen that the conditions in Ladore prior to the arrival of the railroad were not so much due to a failure in the character of the citizenry in general, but due to the existing social structure not being robust enough to withstand the negative "perks" that came along with the railroad construction gangs as the M.K.&T. built southward through Neosho County. Whatever the case, the reputation of Ladore in history was tarnished almost indelibly by the actions of the "newcomers" and "ne'er do-wells" who arrived in the few months prior to the railroad; tarnished so much as to almost obscure what the character and industry of its first citizens had created over a period of two years of building to that point. In any event, in the months prior to the arrival of the M.K.&T. tracks in Ladore, the rough and tumble element that preceded it had created a local situation where drinking, robbery, horse theft and claim jumping were becoming more and more of a problem.

Chapter 3: The Tragedy at Ladore

The affair known as the Ladore Tragedy became a nationally known event.   Newspapers such as the New York *Times*, Philadelphia *Inquirer*, and other newspapers across the country printed versions of the affair, usually picking up the version of the story as printed in the Fort Scott *Monitor*.   People who were in Ladore that night and participated to one degree or another were still recounting the event a half a century later. It has remained part of the folklore of Neosho and Labette counties in southeastern Kansas until the present day.

Taking into consideration the various versions of the story, the basic agreed upon facts in all versions are these. On what would have been the day of May 9 through the early morning of May 10, 1870, a gang of seven men entered the town of Ladore (some versions put the number as high as fourteen members of the gang) and began drinking. While spending the afternoon in Ladore, they accosted and robbed several citizens, reportedly terrorizing the town. Towards the evening, in a search for more drink and a place to stay for the night, they went to Fort Roach to obtain both. James Roach refused them entry. The men then forced themselves into the place, pistol whipping Mr. Roach into unconsciousness and presumed death, kidnapped two serving girls from the place and took them out into the trees near Labette Creek and raped them. The girls' ages were reported as ranging anywhere from 12 years of age to 16 years. Upon regaining consciousness, Mr. Roach went for help to the town. A gang of vigilantes was rounded up (reported to be as many as 300 in number) and the surrounding area searched for the gang members in the early morning of May 10.

One gang member had been shot by another over a dispute over one of the two girls. Two were captured in town. One was found encamped down on the banks of Labette Creek with one of the girls held prisoner. Three were captured on the road to Osage Mission. The six surviving gang members were brought before the two girls for identification. Five of them were identified by the girls and upon identification each was in turn hung from the same limb of a hackberry tree along the bank of the creek. The last surviving member was not hung, having not been identified as a rapist by the girls and was taken into custody when law enforcement had finally arrived on the scene. The five dead members of the gang hung there until the next day, when they were cut down from the tree and buried in a common grave with the member who had been shot under the branches of the hackberry tree from which they had hung.

Woodcut of the Lynching at Ladore, Kansas – 1870
[B7. Masterson, N1. Parsons *Sun*]

These are the basic facts upon which all the various accounts agree; the differences in the account being largely ones of detail. In some versions the gang numbered as many as fourteen. In some versions the girls were daughters of Roach and not servant girls. In some versions the gang was in town to rob the payroll for the railroad workers and the rape of the girls was barely noted. Some versions of the story had the girls near the point of death, and in some the remaining gang member escaped custody.

The rest of this chapter will be spent in exploring the various more local versions of the story, in part to determine which are closer to the fact of what the existing historical record can show, and in part to explore how each helped to form the historical reputation of the town of Ladore.

The Fort Scott *Monitor* Version:

At the time in 1870 this was the most widely circulated news account of the Ladore Tragedy. Most of the newspapers across the country, when picking up the story, either reprinted or based their own story on that which appeared in the Fort Scott *Monitor*. In particular, the version printed in the New York *Times* came from the *Monitor*.

The Osage Mission *Journal* Version:

This version was the first reported and was reported a day earlier than the Neosho Valley *Eagle*, Neosho County *Dispatch* and Fort Scott *Monitor*. The *Eagle* out of Erie and the *Dispatch* and *Journal* out of Osage Mission were the closest towns / papers to the events in Ladore.

The Neosho Valley *Eagle* and Neosho County *Dispatch* Version:

The same version was printed in both papers.

Parsons *Sun* Versions (1920, 1921, 1926, 1938, 1971):

The city of Parsons did not yet exist, nor did the *Sun*, but the 1920 account was from Dr. George Gabriel who lived in Ladore and who was part of the vigilante group, and the 1921 and later versions were obtained from and reprints of that of Mrs. Mary Neely (wife of Capt. M.M. Neely) who lived in Ladore at the time of the event.

Lawrence *Republican Journal* Version:

There were actually two versions printed in this paper. The first was the *Monitor* version with some additional details and the second was filed by the correspondent Wheeler a few days after the event with still more details. A later notice in the paper identified the girls by name.

Southern Kansas *Advance* (Chetopa) Version:

This version differs slightly in some details, but is largely consistent on several of the main points. It is one of the few versions that attribute the gang's presence in Ladore that day for the broader purpose of robbery and gives some corroboration therefore for the Neely version later published in the *Sun*.

L.A. Bowes Version:

Bowes was a foreman for the company contracting to build the railroad for the M.K.&T. and was living in Ladore at the time. His version was first printed in the Topeka *Mail & Breeze* in 1902 and later reprinted in other papers, including the Kansas City *Times* in 1971. It was also quoted in V.V. Masterson's book, *The Katy Railroad and the Last Frontier*. Most accounts are more consistent with his account than otherwise.

Neosho Valley *Register* (Iola) Peter Kelly Version:

This is perhaps the most important version in that it contains information directly from the surviving member of the gang, Peter Kelly, who was in custody in the Allen County Jail in Iola awaiting his appearance in court when interviewed by the *Register*. His version of the events, as they pertain to his actions are corroborated by two or three of the other accounts, independent of his information.

Neosho County District Court #235 – State vs. Peter Kelly:

This is the court transcript for the charges that were actually filed against Peter Kelly and the sequence of events of his initial custody.

For clarity, the details of the various versions are laid out for comparison as follows:

L.A. Bowes Version:

The Gang:	The gang consisted of seven members, named as Patrick Starr, Patsy Riley, Richard Pilbin, Alex Mathews, Robert Wright, and Peter Kelly and supposedly from the Indian Territory. Two were caught in town, three were caught on the road to Osage Mission, one was caught with one of the girls, one (Wright) was shot. The gang arrived on foot.
The Girls:	The two girls were servants working for Mr. Roach. The youngest was 12 years old. Both girls were raped. The extent of any further injury to the girls was not mentioned. The girls were able to identify the specific gang members who had abused them. The girls' names were not mentioned.
Peter Kelly:	One gang member took the younger of the two girls from the situation and got her back to Roach's boarding house. This member survived the hanging and was taken into custody by Sheriff Barnes.
Other Crimes:	The gang spent the day in Ladore in knocking down, accosting and robbing citizens and getting

	drunk. No other prior criminal activity mentioned.
Ft. Roach	Ft. Roach was a double log cabin, two stories tall, with a staircase in the middle. The gang left two members on guard who kept 25 railroad workers lodged upstairs at bay. The gang arrived at the boarding house about 7 p.m. The posse was formed about an hour before dawn. The lynching was over by 11 a.m.

Parsons *Sun* (Mrs. Neely) Version:

The Gang:	The gang had been active in the area for several weeks and had been stealing horses, etc. They came to town to steal the payroll for the railroad workers. Mrs. Neely did not recall the names of the gang members. The gang arrived in ones and twos, loitering around town during the day.
The Girls:	Mrs. Neely's version contended that the gang was in Ladore to steal the payroll. The first printed account did not mention anything about the rape of the girls. The second mentioned the girls, but still emphasized the payroll theft as the main purpose of the gang.
Peter Kelly:	Peter Kelly turned state's evidence and identified a gang of up to 14 members. He was held in custody in Girard.
Other Crimes:	Mrs. Neely contended that the gang had operated up and down the line of construction of the M.K.&T., robbing settlers along the line.
Ft. Roach	Roach's place was disreputable and known for shouting, fighting and drinking. Noises were heard in town, but ignored as they were not considered to be unusual for that place.

Parsons *Sun* (Dr. Gabriel) Version:

The Gang:	The gang consisted of seven members, but he did not name them. Roach came to Dr. Gabriel's residence for help. One gang member was caught with a girl near Labette Creek, two were caught in a house on the west side of town, and three were caught out on the trail in the vicinity of South Mound. One gang member was shot by another gang member.
The Girls:	Dr. Gabriel mentions the one girl, but not two. The extent of injuries was not mentioned and the girl was not named.
Peter Kelly:	Dr. Gabriel stated that the surviving gang member was taken in custody to Erie, but escaped before he was brought to trial.
Other Crimes:	No other crimes that day were mentioned, but Gabriel noted the level of local crime dropped quickly after the lynching took place.
Ft. Roach	Ft. Roach was a double log cabin, two stories tall, with a staircase in the middle and no windows on the second floor. The gang kept 6 railroad workers lodged upstairs at bay by firing guns at them.

Neosho Valley *Eagle* & Neosho County *Dispatch* Version:

The Gang:	The gang consisted of seven members, with none being named. One gang member was shot by another in a dispute over one of the girls.
The Girls:	The two girls were servants working for Mr. Roach, aged 11 and 17. Mr. Roach's daughter escaped through a window. The younger was returned to the house in a "precarious" condition while the elder was "repeatedly outraged" during the night. The girls were not named.

Peter Kelly:	The last gang member was saved by the arrival of the sheriff and was taken into custody, waiting for the next term of district court.
Other Crimes:	The activities of the gang earlier in the day were not mentioned.
Ft. Roach	No description or characterization of the Roach residence was given.

Osage Mission *Journal* Version:

The Gang:	The gang consisted of seven members, named as Patrick Starr, Patsy Riley, Richard Pilbin, Alex Mathews, Robert Wright, and Peter Kelly. The gang arrived at night.
The Girls:	The two girls were servants working for Mr. Roach. The youngest was not yet 12 years old. Both girls were raped. The extent of any further injury to the girls was not mentioned. The girls were able to identify the specific gang members who had abused them. The girls' names were not mentioned.
Peter Kelly:	The survivor was turned over to authorities and held in jail in default of bail at Osage Mission. He was supposedly a former L.L.&G. railroad worker.
Other Crimes:	The gang robbed several citizens and shot guns at others.
Ft. Roach	The gang divided into groups to prevent outside interference and "escape by inmates."

Fort Scott *Monitor* Version:

The Gang:	The gang consisted of seven members, and were presumed to be workers on the Galveston (L.L.&G.) road. One was captured with one of the girls, two captured in town and three captured on the road to Osage Mission. One gang member shot by another member of the gang.

The Girls:	Roach's daughter barely escaped. The two girls were servants and aged 12 and 14. Knives were used and both girls were cut and in critical condition and not expected to survive.
Peter Kelly:	Surviving gang member managed to convince the mob that he was not involved with the rapes. Fate of the surviving gang member not known at time the article was written.
Other Crimes:	The gang spent the day "drinking and carousing."
Ft. Roach	Roach's place described as a boarding house. Hangings were done by noon. Doctors tending the girls.

Lawrence *Republican Journal* Version:

The Gang:	The gang consisted of seven members, who were presumed to be from Texas or the Indian Territory. One was captured with one of the girls, two captured in town and three captured on the road to Osage Mission. One gang member shot by another member of the gang.
The Girls:	Girls originally identified as daughters of Roach, aged 12 and 14. Later notice named the girls as Jane and Alice Talbert, ages 12 and 16.
Peter Kelly:	Surviving gang member in custody of citizens, fate unknown.
Other Crimes:	The gang spent the day "drinking and carousing."
Ft. Roach	Roach's place described as a boarding house.

Southern Kansas *Advance* Version:

The Gang:	The gang consisted of nine members. Two members were left on guard outside Roach's house and left when things got too "high-handed." Of the

	other seven, one was captured with one of the girls, two captured in town and three captured on the road to Osage Mission near the Neosho River. One gang member shot by another member of the gang. The gang was first supposed to be railroad workers, then a gang organized for "robbery and plunder."
The Girls:	The two girls were servants and aged 12 and 14. Knives were used and both girls were "ravished" all night and not expected to survive.
Peter Kelly:	Surviving gang member managed to convince the mob that he was not involved with the rapes. He was put into custody and taken to Osage Mission.
Other Crimes:	Activities of the gang prior to the rapes that day were not mentioned.
Ft. Roach	Roach's place described as a boarding house. The gang arrived at Roach's about 9 p.m. The vigilante mob was formed and the gang members rounded up starting around dawn.

Neosho Valley *Register* (Peter Kelly) Version:

The Gang:	The gang were, or had been, railroad workers. Five members went to the Roach boarding house while two (Mathews and Kelly) went to camp along Labette Creek. Filburn (or Pilburn) claimed to know Roach. Starr, Wright, Pilburn, Riley and Ryan went to Roach's house.
The Girls:	The two girls were "outraged in a most brutal manner." The youngest girl was aged 13. Girls identified all but Kelly as being involved.
Peter Kelly:	Kelly heard shots fired and came back from the camp. Starr had shot Wright. Kelly took the younger girl away from Starr and Wright, who were fighting over her, and returned her to Roach's house. He then took to the trail to Osage Mission and was joined by Riley and Ryan later. The three

	were caught on the trail. Kelly was taken in custody to Osage Mission and later transferred to Iola.
Other Crimes:	The gang spent the day "drinking and carousing."
Ft. Roach	No description of Roach's house.

Neosho County District Court – State Vs. Peter Kelly – Case #235:

The Gang:	Charges filed against Peter Kelly by J.N. Roach for rape of Jane Talbert.
The Girls:	Jane Talbert was named, age stated as "upwards of 10 years."
Peter Kelly:	Transcript shows chain of custody for Kelly between Osage Mission and Iola. Presumably held in custody for trial later in 1871.
Other Crimes:	No other charges were filed against Kelly, so far as has been found.
Ft. Roach	Not applicable, no description given of Roach's house.

Every other published version of the story of the Ladore tragedy so far known has derived from one of these versions; usually from either Bowes' account or the *Monitor's* account.

A few things become apparent when considering the various accounts of the Ladore Tragedy. One is that James N. Roach's style of life and business had not changed much from his days in Fort Scott. The Fort Roach of drinking and long dances and parties at Fort Scott seems consistent with the type of "boarding house and tavern" that he seemed to be running as his new Fort Roach / Ladore. The second point is that there seemed to be a social schism in Ladore between Roach and some of the later settlers. Mrs. Neely attributed the outlaws' reason for being in Ladore to an effort to steal a payroll that, by her own account, no one even knew had been brought into town until after the events were all over and the outlaws hung to a tree. Mrs. Neely's exact quotes from the pages of the Parsons *Sun* of 1926 and 1938 in reference to the events that night and to Fort Roach's place in the community are as follows:

--"About three-quarters of a mile away was a boarding house where most of the men employed on the construction work lived. It was conducted by a man named Roach and was called Fort Roach. It was a disreputable place where it was generally understood liquor was sold."

> - Parsons *Daily Republican,* March 7, 1926, "Wholesale Hanging at Ladore"

From this quote, Mrs. Neely seems to be wanting to point out James Roach and his boarding house as the source of the liquor problem in Ladore. However, Bowes in his account said:

--"Ladore was the toughest place I ever struck. Whiskey was sold in nearly every house tree in town. Vice and immorality flourished like a green bay tree."

> - V.V. Masterson, "The Katy Railroad and the Last Frontier"

Also, Dr. Gabriel in his recollections of the Ladore of 1870 said:

--"I think there were perhaps 1,500 people living there; and there was more pure and undefiled meanness there than any other place for the size of it."

--"You could look up the street at almost any time of the day or night and see from one to half a dozen fights going on."

--"I had ridden down the streets more than once and seen fellows being robbed in the full light of day, almost every house had a saloon in it and those that did not had plenty to drink on the side."

> - Parsons *Sun*, March 19, 1920, "Fifty Years Ago Strange Laws Ruled"

Add to this the statements of the spread of dram shops and the drinking problem in advance of the railroad as described in the Wheeler columns, it is clear that the drinking "scourge" was not just relegated to the boarding house across the road south of the town. It does at least seem possible that Mrs. Neely preferred to remember things otherwise.

Further evidence of a schism and some feeling against Judge Roach by some in Ladore can be inferred from these passages from two profile articles on Ladore, published in the Fort Scott *Monitor* in July of 1870.

--"But don't you think the good people down here claim that Ladore was *always Ladore;* and that it *never was* Fort Roach."

--"The Ladore folks don't appreciate Roach, though the old man's health is still good, and his cheeks are as rosy as ever."

--"Ladore, as you all know, is 'Old Fort Roach.' Every large town in Southern Kansas has had its 'Old Fort Roach;' Ladore has it, and Fort Scott had it, and all of the one-horse towns south of here will have their 'Old Fort Roach' before they amount to much."

- Fort Scott *Monitor*, July 23 and July 28, 1870

Add to this the further comment made by Mrs. Neely in reference to what might have been known or not known in Ladore proper on the night of the Ladore Tragedy:

--"During the night there was a quarrel and one of the visitors was killed. There was much shooting and fighting, but as the place was noted for having an occasional roughhouse the citizens paid no attention to the shooting and screaming which continued until morning."

- Parsons *Daily Republican*, March 7, 1926, "Wholesale Hanging at Ladore"

So, on the one hand in her recollection of the events of that day and night Mrs. Neely attributes the presence of the desperadoes to an attempt to steal a payroll that no one in town even knew was there, if her account is to be believed, and on the other hand while barely acknowledging that two girls were raped, she attributes no responsibility for intervention earlier to the fact that Ft. Roach was "disreputable" and there was no reason to pay attention to "the shooting and screaming which continued until morning." It seems that there might have been some in Ladore who were aware that something was going on that night, but elected instead to turn and look the other way. Is it possible even to the point of creating a story to have the outlaws there for another reason entirely in order to soften some guilt feelings about that night? It certainly wouldn't be the first time such a thing was done by people after a crisis event, and selective memory is a powerful thing.

There is a dichotomy to Mrs. Neely's account of that night. She describes the behavior of the gang of men as they came into Ladore in the following manner:

--"'One day a few quiet looking fellows came into town. They drifted in one or two at a time. Apparently they were day laborers looking for employment. They loafed about the various business places, listening and talking. That night when leaving every man asked if he might leave his carpet bag or bundle. Each said he expected to obtain work and would return later.'"

- Parsons *Daily Republican*, March 7, 1926, "Wholesale Hanging at Ladore"

This account of the gang's activity that day in Ladore, however, gives little reason, other than letting those on the "wrong side" of town alone, for no aid to have been forthcoming, even though there was heard "shooting and screaming until morning." However, most of the other accounts, written in the days following the incident in 1870 or remembered by those participating in the events, paint quite a different picture of the degree to which the citizens of Ladore might have felt safe in lending assistance.

--"That evening about dusk (the seven) began operations by knocking men down and robbing them." Bowes told the Topeka *Mail and Breeze* in 1902. "As they were heavily armed they soon had full possession of the town and everything their own way during the night."

--"An hour or so before dawn, Bowes was asleep in his quarters on Labette Creek, a quarter mile south of Roach's. A dozen men asked him to help capture the desperadoes. As an illustration of how thoroughly Ladore had been cowed, Bowes knew nothing of the siege in town the day before or the night's events."

- Kansas City *Times*, November 25, 1971, "Gang and Greed Dug Town's Grave"
- Topeka *Mail and Breeze*, 1902

--"It seems that on Tuesday night a gang, consisting of seven men, took possession of the town of Ladore, robbed several of the citizens, fired their revolvers at others and "raised the devil" generally. The citizens— who bear the reputation of being civil and orderly—were powerless in the hands of the drunken desperadoes."

- Osage Mission *Journal*, May 12, 1870, "Horrific Tragedy at Ladore"

--"They remained in town during the day drinking and carousing."

- Fort Scott *Monitor*, May 13, 1870, "An Infamous Proceeding"

--"From the *Journal* we learned that during the 10th this gang of desperados had undisputed sway at Ladore, robbing houses and people at pleasure, and keeping the citizens in a state of terror and abeyance by firing their revolvers at them."

- Fort Scott *Monitor*, May 15, 1870, "The Ladore Tragedy"

--"On last Tuesday, the 10th inst., nine devils in human form came to Ladore, Neosho County. They first shot at, and robbed a citizen, then went to the saloon, where they threatened to *run* the town."

- Southern Kansas *Advance*, May 18, 1870, "Horrible Outrage"

From the other accounts of that day, the behavior of the gang ranged from "drinking and carousing" to acts of robbery, violence and shooting at citizens. Based on the accounts then, the gang supposedly for a time that day and night had the "run" of the place and were largely free to do as they wished. How widespread this phenomena was, however, is not certain as in L.A. Bowes' account and Dr. Gabriel's account, neither seemed aware of any of the events particular to that day until word was brought to them later and in Mrs. Neely's account, shooting and screaming were heard, but no action was taken by those who could hear the noises. Apparently then, either the citizens who finally acted didn't know what was happening at Roach's boarding house until after it was over, or elected not to act on what they were hearing, based on that place's unsavory reputation.

At this writing the fate of the Talbert girls is not known. Some of the accounts placed them so near death as a result of their injuries that they were not expected to live. In other versions they were raped, but no statement beyond that fact was made as to their condition afterward. In many of the accounts the villains were brought before the girls so that the girls could positively identify their assailants, which they were apparently physically well enough to do. Charges were ultimately filed only on behalf of Jane Talbert, against Peter Kelly, by James Roach in the office of Justice of the Peace, John Hall, a Ladore resident, on that very same day, May 10th. A search of court records shows no other charges as having been filed. According to the accounts, neither girl identified Kelly as one of their assailants. If one of the girls had in fact died, it would have seemed proper at some point for at least an accessory to murder charge to have been filed.

According to Peter Kelly's version of the event, as told in an interview with the Neosho Valley *Register*, the newspaper in Iola, Kansas, while he was in custody in the Allen County jail, he was never directly involved in either the assault on Mr. Roach, or the rapes of the girls. In fact, according to his version of events he and one other of the gang had elected to camp out on the trail, rather than go to Roach's house. He was informed by one of the gang later that things were getting out of hand at Roach's and came back at that time. Upon arrival there as reported in the *Register*:

--"**on arrival at the house [he] found two of them outside with the youngest girl, trying to ravish her when he interfered and told them it was a shame to treat a young girl thus, took her away from them and put her back into the house.**"

- Neosho Valley Register, May 18, 1870, "Horrible Outrage"

It was about this time that Patrick Starr, one of the gang, shot Robert Wright, another of the gang, in the head in a dispute over the girl. L.A. Bowes' account corroborates Kelly's version, at least to the extent that he (Bowes) stated that one of the gang had gotten the youngest girl away from the rest and returned her to the boarding house. In some of the other accounts it is stated that the surviving gang member (Kelly) managed to convince the mob that he had not been involved in the rapes.

Case #235 – State of Kansas vs. Peter Kelly is the only court record or transcript that has so far been found recording any charges filed in the affair. The record of court action after this occurred in the Tioga *Herald* of July 1, 1871, in a summary of cases coming to trial in the district court that session. Listed on the docket is State vs. Peter Kelly, for rape, and in a bit of historical irony, State vs. J.N. Roach, for assault. This is over a year after the events that night in Ladore. Assuming the charge pertained to the Ladore case, it is not clear as to whether Peter Kelly was in custody all that time, or if he had been released on bail. In either event, the case did not actually come up for trial until December of that year. The trial cases for the winter term of the district court were posted in the Neosho County *Journal* (formerly Osage Mission *Journal*) on December 2, and December 9, 1871. The cases were adjudicated as follows:

-- **District Court:--State vs. Peter Kelly—dismissed on motion of county attorney.**

-- **District Court:--State vs. J.N. Roach—peace recognizance, dismissed on motion of county attorney.**

-- **District Court:--State vs. J.N. Roach (December 16, 1871)—Jury trial, verdict of not guilty.**

> **- Neosho County *Journal*, December 9, December 16, 1871**

This would seem to be the final corroboration of Peter Kelly's version of his involvement in the events that night, in that when it came to trial, the county attorney chose not even to pursue the case beyond recommending the charges be dismissed.

It must be noted, historical irony aside, that the cases involving J.N. Roach did not relate to the events of May 10, 1871. Roach's case involved two separate instances of assault, one verbal, the other with a cane or club, against one James Oldfield. In each case there was a disagreement between the two of some kind, with Roach verbally threatening to have Oldfield run out of town, and apparently at one point using a club or cane to emphasize his point. This incident, though he ultimately was acquitted of the charges, cannot help but to add more color to an already colorful life for Mr.

Roach. The State vs. J.N. Roach cases were #396 and #397 in the court records. As a final note, there was a notice of a sheriff's sale of Mr. Oldfield's cattle in front of M.M. Neely's drug store, for failure to pay court costs in this matter.

An attempt at a final comment and an epitaph for the Ladore Tragedy was written as a poem by Col. J.W. Horner of Chetopa, Kansas owner and publisher of the Southern Kansas *Advance* of June 1, 1870, entitled "The Fall of Ladore."

The Fall of Ladore

Ladore is a little town on the Missouri, Kansas & Texas railroad. Its whisky saloons are said to outnumber their places of business.

How does the whisky
Go down at Ladore?

In punches and julips,
'Twixt every man's two lips,
In Thomas and Jerries,
In villainous sherries,
In clarets concocted,
Of legwood and rot-gut,
In smiles and smashes,
It pours and it dashes,
In forty-rod lightning,
Each poor sucker tight'ning,
In hot stings and toddies,
Befuddling the Paddies,

In straight drinks of strychnine,
And—'ades with a stick in,
In drinks before daylight,
In drinks til the midnight,
In drinks between drinks, o'er and o'er,
OH! How *does* the whisky go down at Ladore!

In cataracts roaring,
From demi-johns pouring,
From glasses o'erflowing,
'Mid swearing and tearing,
And fighting and smiting,
Sad sight to delight in!
'Mid brawling and falling, and crawling,
And sprawling like swine in the sties,
They bludgeon, and blacken, and bung out their eyes,
And call for more drinks, till their gullets are sore,
Oh Lord! But the whisky goes down at Ladore.

For leagued with the Devil,
Old Bacchus holds revel,
And each broth of Finnegan,
Fills up the can again,
And 'mid such confusion as niver ye saw,
They guzzle and swig to old Erin-go-bragh,
And keep it up daily, the sprigs of shelalah,
Til clenching and creeping and gasping,
And raw with their terrible rasping,
Till belted and pelted and welted,
And battered and tattered and shattered,
And bloated and blear-eyed and blizzard,
And scalloped and walloped and scissored,
And burned out from touch-hole to gizzard,

And busted from A doyen to lizzard,
The Devil has no use for them more,
And has struck from his ledger the name of Ladore.

The historical story of Ladore as printed in the history books available for that era is consistent with the poem. The narrative that is found when one looks has the entirety of Ladore as a wild, wicked, western town whose wickedness had brought upon it a just fate. However, there was more to Ladore than just that one terrible night in May, 1870 and the events that had led to it. Prior to that night, Ladore was much like any newly developing town. After that night Ladore for a time was a major political center in the most formative event for both Neosho and Labette counties. The event was the years long legal struggle between the settlers and the L.L.&G. and M.K.&T. railroad companies, and it is a struggle largely forgotten by the residents of the two counties today. The struggle embodied themes such as class struggle, political rings and monoply, and corporate influence in government affairs that defined the late 19th and early 20th centuries as the "Gilded Age," and resonates even into the 21st century economic and the ideological struggles that define the political arena in the United States today.

Chapter 4: Settlers vs. Railroads – Birth of the S.P.A.

Ladore as a Political Center:

In geographical location, being just a couple of miles north of the Neosho County - Labette County line and almost dead center from east to west, Ladore was almost at the center point of the Osage Ceded Lands. This made it an attractive place for meetings of settlers in the early period of settlement. Its placement on the main state road and future location on the main rail line that would pass through the center of the two counties added to its convenience as a meeting place in 1870.

The political situation with respect to land claims on the Osage Ceded Lands was basically a competition between two competing land grants between two different railroads, the L.L.&G. and the M.K.&T., and a series of treaties negotiated between the United States and the Osage Indians, defining the extent of the Osage Reservation in Kansas Territory / the State of Kansas over a period from 1825 until 1870. The full details of this battle would make a book in and of itself. The particulars of the situation and how Ladore was involved will be summarized here.

In 1825 two treaties were negotiated with the Osage Indians, redefining the territory of their reservation and moving them out of their territories in Arkansas, Missouri, and what would become the state of Oklahoma. The graphic below shows an overlay of the approximate extent of the reservation on the modern state of Kansas. In 1825, what would become Kansas Territory and later the state of Kansas was merely a part of the central region of the Louisiana Purchase.

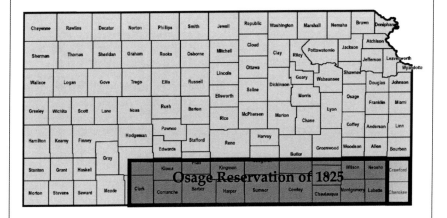

Osage Treaty of 1825

The map above shows the approximate extent of the Osage Reservation after the ratification of the Osage Treaty of 1825. Also indicated on the east end are the Cherokee Neutral Lands. The base map is from agriculture.ks.gov.

The Treaty of 1825:

➢ The Grand and Little Osage ceded their lands in Missouri and the Arkansas Territory to the United States.

➢ The Grand and Little Osage ceded "all lands lying West of the said State of Missouri and Territory of Arkansas, North and West of the Red River, South of the Kansas River, and East of a line to be drawn from the head sources of the Kansas, Southwardly through the Rock Saline **[W10. Osage Treaty of 1825]**."

➢ The United States, from this section of land, created a reservation 50 miles wide north and south and starting 25 miles west of the Missouri state line running to the western boundary defined from the Kansas River head waters to the Rock Saline. These lands were reserved for occupation and use by the Osage for "so long as they may choose to occupy the same."

➢ The United States reserved rights to navigation on the streams and waterways of the reservation and the right to appoint Indian agents, teachers, and instructors. The second treaty, also concluded in 1825, gave the United States the right to build free access roads through the reservation.

➢ The United States would pay the tribe a sum of $7,000 (or the equivalent in goods and materials) per year for a total of 20 years. The tribe would also be given various livestock, farming equipment and supplies, and dwellings would be built for the four principal chiefs of the tribe.

➢ 54 one square mile tracts would be laid off at the discretion of the President of the United States and sold to finance the building of schools for the children of the tribe.

The phrase "so long as they may choose to occupy the same", became an important arguing point in the 1870's as the settlers on the Osage Ceded Lands made their case against the railroad companies in their battles over the land claims.

The Osage Reservation remained as defined by the 1825 treaty during the time of the creation of Kansas Territory by the Kansas Nebraska Act in 1854, during the time of the creation of the pre-emption and homestead laws and through the course of the Civil War.

In 1854, after the acts creating the territories of Kansas, Nebraska and New Mexico had been drafted and passed, a second act that established the position of a surveyor-general for these territories was passed on July 22nd. Section 12 would prove to be important to the settlers of southeast Kansas in the 1870's. The enabling act of July 22nd, 1854 organized the survey of the territories of Kansas and Nebraska out of the Louisiana Purchase. The law is titled "An Act to Establish the Offices of Surveyor-General of New Mexico, Kansas, and Nebraska, to Grant Donations to Actual Settlers Therein, and for Other Purposes, [10 Stat 308]" and section 12 of the statute reads:

> Sec. 12. *And be it further enacted*, That all the lands to which the Indian title has been or shall be extinguished within said Territories of Nebraska and Kansas, shall be subject to the operations of the Preemption Act of fourth September, eighteen hundred and forty-one, and under the conditions, restrictions, and stipulations therein mentioned; *Provided, however*, That where unsurveyed lands are claimed by preemption, notice of the specific tracts claimed shall be filed within three months after the survey has been made in the field, and on the failure to file such notice or to pay for the tracts claimed before the day fixed for the public sale of the lands by the proclamation of the President of the United States, the parties claiming such lands shall forfeit all right thereto; *Provided*, said notices may be filed with the Surveyor-General, and to be noted by him on the township plats, until other arrangements shall have been made by law for that purpose.

The statute made the Indian lands in Kansas subject to pre-emption in 1854. Later treaties notwithstanding, the legal precedent would be that, whenever a tribe would extinguish their claim to their reserved lands in Kansas, the lands would be opened up for pre-emption (and later homesteading) so long as notice of claim was filed within a period of time once the survey of the land into sections and quarter sections had been accomplished.

In 1861, just as the Civil War was beginning, the territory of Kansas entered the Union as the 34th State. Even during the Civil War, Congress was considering the future development of the new states to be carved out of the Louisiana Purchase and would pass laws to aid in internal improvements in these newly formed states. For the State of Kansas, it was the following act:

The Kansas Land Grand Act of 1863 – 12 Stat. 772, Ch. 98

THIRTY-SEVENTH CONGRESS, Sess. III, Ch. 98, 1863   Page 772

March 8, 1863: Chapter 98; An Act for a Grant of Lands to the State of Kansas, in alternate Sections, to aid in the Construction of certain Railroads and Telegraphs in said State.

From this act would be created railroads that most Kansans would know, the Atchison, Topeka and Santa Fe (the Santa Fe R.R.), the Leavenworth, Lawrence & Gulf (later Galveston) (the L.L.&G. R.R.), and the Missouri, Kansas & Texas (the M.K.&T. or "Katy" R.R.) among others. The Kansas Legislature, in accordance with this statute, would create grants of land within the borders of Kansas for the L.L.&G. R.R. in 1864 and for the M.K.&T. in 1866 during the time when that company was still known as the Union Pacific – Southern Branch R.R. The basic provisions for these grants was that the railroad companies would be granted the odd numbered sections of land on either side of their rail lines, for a distance of 10 miles on each side. When at a later date the railroads tried to press these claims to all sections whether they were even or odd-numbered making no difference, the railroads were effectively trying to claim almost all the land that would later become available in both Neosho and Labette counties.

The following maps on the next two pages show the extent of the problem for settlers and railroad companies attempting to claim lands in the Osage Ceded Lands.

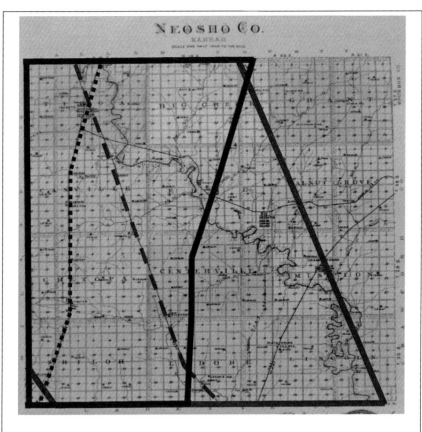

MK&T Land Grant in Neosho County

LL&G Land Grant in Neosho County

Approximate extent of the land grants for the L.L.&G. railroad (blue) and M.K.&T. railroad (red) in Neosho County, Kansas. The land grant was initially given as the odd numbered sections on either side of the line of the road for 10 miles on either side. Each square on the map is a one square mile section.

At a later date, the companies tried to make the case for both even and odd sections, affecting practically every township in the county and almost all of the land that would come open for settlement.

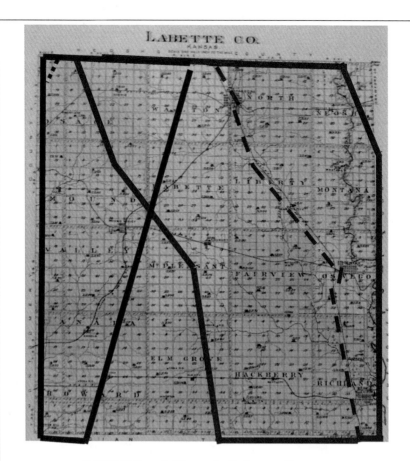

MK&T Land Grant in Labette County

LL&G Land Grant in Labette County

Approximate extent of the land grants for the L.L.&G. railroad (blue) and M.K.&T. railroad (red) in Labette County, Kansas. The land grant was initially given as the odd numbered sections on either side of the line of the road for 10 miles on either side. Each square on the map is a one square mile section.

At a later date, the companies tried to make the case for both even and odd sections, affecting practically every township in the county and almost all of the land that would come open for settlement.

Complications caused by the land grant legislation included the lack of provision for deciding competing claims between the companies should the grants overlap (which they decidedly did in Neosho and Labette counties), the existence of the enabling act in 1854 which gave settlers pre-emption rights that preceded the existence of the grants of 1864 and 1866, and the fact that the lands in Neosho and Labette counties were still part of the existing Osage Reservation, and were not under the jurisdiction of the Kansas Legislature to give to companies in the nature of grants. The next complication was created when the Osage Treaty of 1865 (also known as the Canville Treaty) was negotiated, creating the Osage Ceded Lands (which at that time was effectively the as not yet split Neosho County).

The Canville Treaty of 1865:

➢ "The tribe of the Great and Little Osage Indians, having now more lands than are necessary for their occupation, and all payments from the Government to them under former treaties having ceased, leaving them greatly impoverished, and being desirous of improving their condition by disposing of their surplus lands"…negotiated a smaller reserve **[W9. Canville Treaty (Osage Treaty of 1865)]**.

➢ The Osage Ceded Lands were ceded (this was Neosho County, Kansas-later split into Neosho and Labette Counties, and a small strip along the eastern edges of what became Montgomery and Wilson Counties).

➢ The United States would pay the Osage tribe $300,000 for the Ceded Lands. The money would be placed on account in the treasury and interest at the rate of 5% in cash or equivalent value in goods and materials would be paid to the tribe semi-annually until the lands were sold.

➤ The United States would sell the lands for cash at the rate established for sale of other public lands. Any money in excess of the $300,000 would go into a "civilization fund" for the general Indian tribes. Cost of surveying and selling the lands would be deducted from the money held on account for the Osage.

➤ No pre-emption or homestead claims were to be recognized except for any settlers already on the lands at the time of the creation of the treaty; who would be able to claim a quarter section based on the survey at $1.25 per acre.

➤ There was language (an amendment) that concerned grants to the state of Kansas to aid in railroad construction (this caused many problems later). A later article gave the railroads the right of way only (upon compensation to the tribe) through reserved lands.

➤ The Osage Trust Lands, running the east-west length of the remaining reservation and extending 20 miles south of the northern boundary, were created. The United States was to survey and sell these lands for cash at no less than $1.25 per acre. The money from this sale would go to the credit of the Osage and the interest (again 5% in cash or equivalent goods, stock and materials) would be given to the Indians each year. Money from the sale would also go into a school fund for the Indians.

The remaining Diminished Reserve Lands were to be occupied by the Osage under the same terms as the 1825 Treaty. If and when they would elect to leave these lands for the Indian Territory (the future Oklahoma), the Diminished Reserve Lands were to be sold under the same terms as established for the Osage Trust Lands. Fifty percent of the proceeds of this sale would be used to procure lands in the Indian Territory.

The Osage (Canville) Treaty of 1865 – The Osage Ceded Lands, the Osage Trust Lands, and the Osage Diminished Reserve

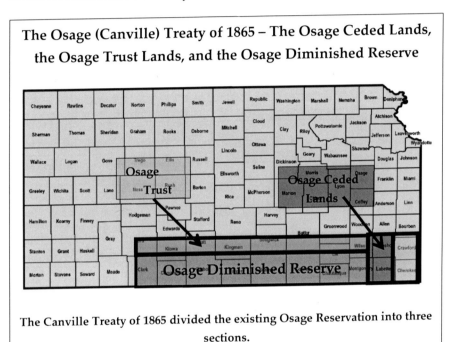

The Canville Treaty of 1865 divided the existing Osage Reservation into three sections.

The legal issues created with this treaty were numerous, one point being that since the treaty wasn't legally active until 1867, the Osage Reservation was not yet split, and the land was not open for grants by the Kansas Legislature. Another issue is that the provision preventing pre-emption and homesteading in the Canville Treaty was in contradiction to the 1854 law earlier mentioned. Then, in 1868, the L.L.&G. tried to negotiate an exclusive treaty with the Osage to get all the Osage lands at $0.19

per acre (The Sturges Treaty). This treaty was withdrawn before it could be ratified and would have been a historic land swindle. Legislation was passed in 1869 to try to correct the problems, but was intentionally misinterpreted by some of the land officers to favor the railroads. Then legislation was enacted and a treaty written in 1870 that made provision for the final removal of the Osage from Kansas to the Indian Territory (now Oklahoma). This had the effect of removing the Indian obstacle to settlement and made settlers and railroad companies even more anxious to enter the former Osage Lands to begin settlement and development of the now open lands.

Thus by the middle of 1870 the situation in the Osage Ceded Lands was chaotic for both the railroad companies and the settlers. By this time some of the settlers had been on their lands for up to 10 years, and had added developments such as houses, barns, farms, fences, wells and so forth. During all this time they had not been able to file claims on their lands due to the legal disputes created between the land grants and the treaties. When a settler would try to file, the railroads would challenge their right to claim. Those already on the land would refuse to leave. New settlers were in a quandary as to whether to buy from the railroads or try to pre-empt or homestead. Those that tried to pre-empt or homestead might find their claim jumped by another settler trying to buy from the railroad companies, or vice versa. The railroad companies, in turn, would try to charge settlers already on the disputed lands prices as high as $8 to $12 per acre, rather than the $1.25 pre-emption/homestead rate, or another rate based upon a later survey, using the value added by the improvements made to the land; improvements the settler himself had built over a period of years.

The situation was unpalatable for both settler and railroad. Neither could proceed to develop the land in the two counties while the other was challenging the legality of their claim. The effect was a retardation of the development of the lands and the slowing down of settlement as incoming settlers would go westward in areas of the former Osage Reserve that were not under legal challenge. The railroads by late 1870 and early 1871 had been built all the way down to the Indian Territory border, the companies had mortaged themselves based on the expected value of their land grants to finance the quick construction they had undertaken, and were soon to go into receivership. Some resolution of the dispute had to occur for both sides to survive economically. The settlers, the companies, and all the people who had come and helped set up towns on the disputed lands all depended upon a legal settlement of the land question.

Ladore, for the time it was still in existence in 1870, became a political center for these issues and demonstrated a situation that was true for most towns in the two counties. The settlers and the townspeople all wanted and needed the railroads to come through their areas, and would be willing to work for them to do so or help form companies themselves to build roads; but while the land dispute was going on, they would also become focal points for resistance to the companies based on the land grant question. During the remainder of 1870 after the Ladore Tragedy had occurred, both were true for Ladore. On the one hand town leaders were promoting the value of Ladore as a junction point for the two divisions of the M.K.&T. R.R. and petitioning the company to be that place, while at the same time the town was hosting settlers' meetings to discuss the land issue and became the place where the organization that did the most to resist the railroads on the land issue was created, the Settlers' Protective Association.

After all that had happened to that point, it was a notice posted in the southeast Kansas newspapers that became a focal point toward galvanizing the organization of another settlers' meeting. It was posted in late May of 1870. Reply to be given, ironically enough, to railroad representatives headquartered in Ladore. The notice was posted in the Osage Mission *Journal* on June 2nd, in the Southern Kansas *Advance* on June 13th, the Neosho County *Dispatch* on June 24th, and in other papers. It read as follows:

To Settlers on Osage Ceded Lands

All persons on EVEN sections of railroad lands will have thirty days from date in which to come up to the principal Land Office at Neosho Falls and buy the same at the appraised value, or else give place to others *who will buy.*

No breaking up of quarter sections. Applications must be made for lands in square quarters.

For further particulars apply to Hurd & Whitney, Ladore, Neosho Co., KS.

ISAAC T. GOODNOW
Land Commissioner,
M.K.&T. R.W. Co.

The emphasis on the word "even" is significant in that the land grants to the railroad companies sought to award the odd-numbered sections for ten miles on either side of the line of the road, with this notice the M.K.&T. sought to claim the even-numbered sections as well. The papers reacted:

--"We consider the above notice as being an outrage on the settlers, and exceedingly faulty in spirit.—Who are the 'High Mightinesses' of the M.K.&T. R.W. Co., that speak in such sharp and autocratic tone, bidding all persons to come up and buy lands on which they are settled, within 30 days, at appraised value or 'else give place to others who will buy.'"

--"Another notice or two like this would make 'all persons' among such settlers come up in 30 days (or less) and administer a salutary lesson to such haughty-toned monopolists as would learn them to treat settlers and others decently in official intercourse."

- Osage Mission *Journal*, June 2, 1870, "Railroad Lands"

--"We are advised that there is considerable feeling among the settlers about the lands claimed by the M.K.&T. R.R. in view of the recent 'Notice' given by the land agents at Ladore."

--"We considered this a very extraordinary notice, arrogant in tone, and unaccommodating in spirit, and such an one as would beget ill-will on the part of those affected by it."

--"Such a spirit is already evoked; and there is a probability that 'Leagues' may be formed and an era of opposition to the Railroad and its claims ushered in."

- Osage Mission *Journal*, June 16, 1870, "The M.K.&T. R.R. Lands"

--"That the above should create an intense feeling of disgust and ill will, not only in the minds of those who are actually settled upon the sections in question, but of all who are interested in the general welfare of this county, towards the railroad corporation and whose behalf it is issued, is by no means extraordinary."

--"When we take into further consideration the fact that the lands have been assessed in a majority of instances at from $8 to $10 per acre, one's feelings arise to a heat other than moderate, and he is very apt to express himself in language more vigorous than elegant."

Neosho County *Dispatch*, June 24, 1870, "Railroad Lands"

While the *Journal* and the *Dispatch* were expressing the outrage being felt by settlers in the disputed areas, each called for moderation. The *Journal* fearing violence and lawlessness should "Land Leagues" be formed, called for the formation of a citizen's committee to meet with the railroad companies and seek a common solution. The *Dispatch* seconded the *Journal's* concerns. The response was to call for a general settlers' meeting over the Fourth of July Holiday, at Ladore, in Dickerson's Grove west of the town.

Speakers such as Gov. Harvey, John Speer, Sidney Clarke, and H.C. Whitney were invited. The meeting was planned for two days, the first day being a traditional celebration of Independence Day and the second for speeches and discussion on the land question between the railroad companies and the settlers. Notices and columns about the meeting would be found in the various newspapers in the weeks before the meeting. The "land question" topic of which Wheeler in his column had written of in a fairly disparaging manner a few weeks before would now start to swing the other direction. By this time the question of purchasing land on the Osage Trust was settled. The bill and resultant treaty to settle the issue in the Diminished Reserve and move the Osage from Kansas into the Indian Territory was passing through Congress. Only in the Osage Ceded Lands was the question of railroad claim at loggerhead with the pre-emption and homestead rights of the settlers.

Newspapers in region and in northern Kansas would print articles in anticipation of the meeting day in Ladore. Themes such as the small, noble settler versus voracious railroad monopoly would be continually invoked to frame the issue in the manner that the settlers wished to have it discussed. Formational themes for the United States, such as liberty and freedom from oppressive government and oppressive land monopoly would be the basis of the grab for the heartstrings of the populace in the Osage Ceded Lands in order to solicit their approval and attendance at the big meeting in Ladore on Independence Day.

'76   '70

GRAND

CELEBRATION

AND

CONVENTION!

Of the Settlers on the Osage Lands, on

July 4 & 5,

AT LADORE

Osage Mission *Journal*, June 9, 1870

--"The gathering at Ladore, in Neosho County, will be one of the largest and most important in Kansas. The call says that it will be a meeting 'whereat the pressing and urgent subject of land titles will be considered.'"

--"In this assembly will be the businessmen of this enterprising new country, the men of means and energy, and the poor squatter from the humblest cabin. It will be emphatically a people's celebration and a people's meeting."

- Kansas *Daily Tribune* (Lawrence), June 14, 1870, "The Gathering at Ladore"

--"Come one, come all, with two days' rations. Object, consideration of land titles."

- Kansas *Daily Tribune* (Lawrence), June 14, 1870, "Great Public Meeting"

--"The meeting at Ladore, on the 4th and 5th bids fair to be the largest ever held in Southern Kansas."

-Osage Mission *Journal*, June 30, 1870, "July 4 & 5 At Ladore"

Up to this point in time, opposition to the policy of railroad land grant claims, the appraisal policies of the land in the contested areas, and legislative opposition had been fairly uncoordinated. Newspaper editors in the region were fairly split, and would continue to be for some time, depending on what they perceived their interest or their community interest to be. Most called for conciliation; on the one hand calling on the railroad companies to lower the appraisal prices and on the other for the settlers to give in and buy from the companies. Legislators from Kansas would try to find solutions amenable to both sides, and would be accused of corruption as a result. Many of the settlers simply couldn't give in. It was all they could do to settle on a quarter-section of land, get a shelter built, make improvements, finance getting a crop in, harvest the crop and transport it to market and still have enough money when the time came to pay the pre-emption price of $1.25 per acre. They were being told they had legal right to $1.25 per acre, not $2, not $4, or $8 or higher. With the meeting at Ladore, the settlers were becoming more organized and would lay the foundation for further organized resistance. Another meeting would be held later in the year where the structure would be put in place, and then for several years several calls for mass meetings on the subject of the land issue and the railroads would become more and more the norm.

What was done at the meeting? What happened and what was the effect? The following excerpts give some information as to these questions.

--"The meeting was a big thing—Professor Bellamy of the county orated, and as everybody expected, did exceedingly well."

--"After dinner Major Whitney, late P.M.U.S.A. spoke a piece. Good order was maintained during the day, and the meeting generally was a credit to Southern Kansas."

--"We met among other celebrities John Speer, the veteran editor and family; they seemed much pleased with the county and people."

--"On the 5th, Major Whitney, late P.M.U.S.A., made another speech, likewise J. Speer. The speeches were well received."

-Osage Mission *Journal*, July 7, 1870, "The 4th at Ladore"

--"In the afternoon the meeting was addressed by H.C. Whitney, Esq. of Humboldt, in political matters generally. He was followed by John Speer, Esq. in an able and well received speech containing a good deal of sound advice to the settlers of Southern Kansas. It was evident from the manner of his reception that the settlers appreciate his constant advocacy of their rights."

--"The meeting on the 5th, although not so large, was, nevertheless, composed of men that were anxious not only to know their rights, but, also, to maintain them. They were addressed at great length by Major Whitney, on the land question."

--"He gave special attention to land question in Neosho and Labette counties, and showed satisfactory that there are good grounds for believing that the settlers on the lands and counties, now claimed by railroad companies, can beat the aforesaid companies in law if they only contest the case as they ought."

--"The settlers then organized a land league, and appointed an executive committee of nine to call meetings in every township in Neosho and Labette counties, and urge all the settlers to join the league, and thus enable themselves to stand up for their rights before the law."

--"An address to the people of the United States on the land question was also adopted. Also a set of resolutions expressive of the sentiment of the meeting on the main issues involved."

Osage Mission *Journal*, July 7, 1870, "The 4th and 5th at Ladore"

The second day's meeting was by far the more devoted to the land issues and settlers' rights, while the meeting on the 4th was the celebration of Independence Day. The basic points of the settlers' legal case against the railroads were being articulated and communicated to large groups of people on the land. The basic organization of opposition to the railroad companies, and at that point government policy as well, was being organized and the decision being made to seek legal, not violent redress of their grievances.

Depending on the paper, the size of the meeting varied. The *Daily Kansas Tribune* (Speer) in its report of the meeting on July 9, 1870 reported an attendance of 6,000 people. It gave a detailed account of the events each day and the names of the people who had organized the meeting and the entertainments. The *Tribune* also printed John Speer's speech in its entirety in its July 12, 1870 report on the meeting as well. The Columbus *Working Man's Journal*, the Kansas *Democrat* (of Oswego), and the Emporia *News* in papers dated July 15th and July 21st printed similar reports of the meeting, stating an attendance of "at least 5,000 persons." While they did not give as much detail to the proceedings as did the *Daily Tribune*, they all printed in their entirety the resolutions passed at the meeting, which are reported below.

"Whereas, By a treaty with the Osages proclaimed in January 1867, it was provided that the lands since known as the "Osage Ceded" lands should be sold for cash; which treaty the Commissioner of the General Land Office authoritatively decided did not vest any title therein, in land monopolies;

And whereas, a Joint Resolution of April 10, 1869, provided for the sale of all said lands to actual settlers at $1.25 per acre;

And whereas, said treaty and decision of the Commissioner of the General Land Office and Joint Resolution have been set at naught by a mere arbitrary ruling of a late Secretary made upon an *ex parte* application of the land monopolies and based upon a mistake of precedent;

And whereas, our right to our homes and our *all* is menaced by said monopolies;

Now, therefore, be it resolved,

That we will contest for our homes under the Joint Resolution aforesaid to the extreme limit of the law; and to secure this end we will organize thoroughly and with discipline, so as to bring the entire material and moral force of the whole array of settlers to bear throughout the contest.

Resolved, That the settlers are hereby solemnly warned not to squander their means in the purchase of an illegal and void monopoly title to their homes, which title must, sooner or later, be overthrown; but they are each and all earnestly entreated to join the settlers' organization, and obtain a title from the general government which shall be cheap, staunch and unmistakable.

Resolved, That we hereby appoint the following temporary Executive Committee, viz: Col. W.H. Carpenter, Geo. T. Walton, Lewis A. Reese, Wm. S. Irwin, Peter Collins, Van Henderleiter, M.H. Sheldon, I.M. Richardson and A.S. Spaulding; and said committee is hereby requested to form and promulgate to the settlers, for their consideration, a plan of permanent organization to secure the object of these resolutions, and until a permanent Executive Committee is formed, to adopt such measures as may be essential to promote the interests of the settlers, and that said committee is requested to prepare an address to the settlers and publish the same immediately.

Resolved, That the settlers are hereby requested immediately to assemble in neighborhood meetings; each neighborhood to select a good and true man, competent to serve as a member of a permanent Executive Committee; and the temporary Executive Committee are requested to select from said list nine members in such manner as that all localities in the ceded lands shall be represented, and said selection shall constitute the permanent Executive Committee for one year from the date of organization.

Resolved, That from this time henceforth "WE MEAN BUSINESS!" and upon our efforts to save our homes we invoke the just consideration of all true men, and the gracious favor of Almighty God!

Yours &c., Van Henderleiter."

From the resolutions the depth of feeling of the settlers and the degree of their commitment can be seen. The fact that they actually accomplished what they set out to do in both the short and long term testifies that these resolutions were no mere statement from a few in an isolated locality; but that they were a statement representing much of the feeling all across the Osage Ceded Lands. The Settlers' Protective Association was born that day, although not yet named. Its ultimate goal, the ability of any settler to file their claim with the government at pre-emption rates as called for in the 1865 Canville Treaty and the 1869 Joint Resolution, was clear. The means to be adopted were not yet set in stone, for much is possible "to the extreme limit of the law." The mandate, however, was clear. Do not buy from the railroads. Do organize to contest for the title to the lands at pre-emption rates. What the S.P.A. would become, now wide it would actually spread its influence and in what manner it would operate (violently or non-violently) was not yet clear, but the birthing ceremony took place at Ladore, and the resolutions were passed.

The next step was taken in a meeting held at Ladore during the week of August 13, 1870. As reported in the *Daily Kansas Tribune,* the constitution and by-laws for the organization were drafted at that meeting to be passed out and debated and voted in a series of mass meetings to be held through the month of September. In the meantime, large political meetings were scheduled in Ladore, Osage Mission and Erie over August 22nd and 23rd at which candidates for state and federal election who were perceived to be friendly to the settlers' cause would speak. Among them were Sidney Clarke, Judge Markham (who was functioning as a lobbyist for the settlers), J.C. Blair and C.G. Burton.

The schedule for the mass meetings to go over the bylaws, the platform, and further discussion of the land question was announced early in September and printed in the papers of the area. The Neosho County *Dispatch* of September 9th, for example, gave the schedule as Ladore, Tuesday September 6, 2 P.M.; Jacksonville, Friday September 9, 7 P.M.; and Erie, Saturday September 10, 2 P.M. The push for attendance was stated as follows, and named the Settler's Protective Association as the organization.

--"All settlers and their friends, who have any interest in the important subject of Settlers' Titles, are urged to be present in force.

By order of the Settlers' Protective Association.

William S. Irwin, Pres.
George S. Walton, Sec."

Neosho County *Dispatch*, September 9, 1870, "Mass Meetings!"

Based on the articles and the reporting at the time, the strategy of the S.P.A. was threefold. First, to test and challenge the railroad land grants in court wherever and whenever possible and to secure funding to pursue the legal case in court. Second, to recommend, and if possible enforce, a mandate that no settler on the Osage Ceded Lands would seek to secure their claim or patent of title from the railroads, but instead seek their title through pre-emption or homesteading. Third, the Association would seek to put up or support candidates for state and federal office and solve the problem through legislative action.

The Neosho County *Dispatch* reported the results of the settlers' meeting in Erie that occurred on September 10th in its September 16th issue. The delegates at the meeting put forth a set of candidates for the following offices: W.S. Irwin, Representative; J.L. Fletcher, Probate Judge; John Brunt, District Court Clerk; C.W. Hayden, Superintendent of Public Instruction. There was no nomination for County Attorney.

The same article in the *Dispatch* also included the results of the settler's meeting held at Ladore on September 6th. This report was also printed in the Oswego *Register* of September 9th and the Osage Mission *Journal* and Labette *Sentinel* of September 22nd. The meeting at Ladore essentially completed the organization of the "Secret Brotherhood of the Settlers' Protective Association of the Osage Ceded Lands" or just the Settlers' Protective Association for short, and published its platform as a resolution. The platform was as follows:

SETTLERS' PROTECTIVE PLATFORM.

Whereas, we, the settlers on the "Osage Ceded Lands" in the State of Kansas believe that under the treaty by which the said lands were ceded to the United States, and under the joint resolutions of Congress, April

10, 1869, actual settlers are entitled to purchase any part of said lands in tracts not to exceed 160 acres, at $1.25 per acre, and that no Corporation has acquired any vested rights therein; and whereas, certain railroad corporations are claiming certain portions of said lands, now therefore:

Resolved,

First, that we will proceed at once to test the validity of said claims, by instituting legal proceedings in the proper courts.

Second, that we respectfully request the Governor of our State to withhold all patents from said corporations for said lands until the termination of said proceedings.

Third, that we will support no candidate for county and legislative offices who is not thoroughly identified with the settlers and in sympathy with their cause.

Fourth, that we are in favor of a judicious and economical management of our county, State and national affairs.

Fifth, that we are opposed to all legislation designed to build up monopolies at the expense of the common people; but that we are in favor of restricting by law their powers within due bounds, and prohibiting the consolidation of all companies having control and management of parallel competing lines of railways.

Sixth, that the federal tariff and revenue laws should be so adjusted as not to be prejudicial to the industrial interest of any section of our country, while securing to our home producers fair competition with foreign capital and labor.

Seventh, that we are opposed to the policy of granting any portions of the public domain to railroad and other corporations, that in case of all such grants, ample provisions should be made for securing their sale at moderate prices and their occupancy upon fair and liberal terms to actual settlers, and that the purchaser's title thereto be derived directly from the Federal Government.

The meeting requests that the State papers copy the resolutions of the convention.

From these initial meetings there were a series of local meetings in the major towns in the Ceded Lands. The New Chicago *Transcript* (in what would later become Chanute, KS) in its September 30th issue reported that the local organizational meeting of its chapter of the S.P.A. had occurred on September 24th. As a measure of the unifying character of the land issue, it was announced at that meeting that S.E. Beach was appointed president of the local association and George C. Crowther, vice-president. What makes this worth noting is that S.E. Beach was a founder of the competing town of Tioga, just immediately to the northwest across the L.L.&G. tracks from New Chicago, and Crowther was editor of the *Transcript* in New Chicago, and the two men were political enemies, Beach being often targeted for negative press in the *Transcript*. It would take almost two more years before the towns would merge to form Chanute.

As the local chapters were getting organized, the S.P.A. began to seek to identify any instances of contested claims by posting notices in the various papers requesting names, addresses and land descriptions of such claims be sent to the Association. From this list the Association could start picking cases to take to court, and to seek to enforce on a local basis the claims of its members against any attempt to jump such claims by those buying from the railroads. An example of a notice is shown below wherein the S.P.A. would seek to determine suitable cases for legal action against one or the other of the railroad companies. This recreation of such a notice was posted in the Labette *Sentinel* of October 27, 1870:

Through the months of September and October, meetings were called for across Labette and Neosho counties as the S.P.A. would send speakers on the land issue and push for the organization of the local chapters. The Labette *Sentinel* reported a schedule of meetings in Labette County for Montana and Labette City on October 28th, Timber Hill on October 29th, and Mound Valley on October 29th. In Neosho County chapters were formed in Thayer, New Chicago – Tioga, Osage Mission, Erie, and Ladore.

Before turning back more to the history and fate of Ladore in 1870, the following remark must be made. The organization and process began in Ladore in 1870 did spread all through the Osage Ceded Lands. The organization carried on its legal challenges to the L.L.&G. and M.K.&T. railroad companies for the next six years while also setting up a "Grand Council" to which its members, in cases where their claims were being contested or outright jumped, would appeal. The S.P.A. was strong enough in many cases to step in and enforce by vigilantism, either threatened or actual, the claims of its members against those settlers seeking to purchase and occupy lands from the railroads. Local law and order notwithstanding, the S.P.A. operated rather openly in this regard, and was rarely prosecuted. The legal battle culminated in a victory in the Federal District Court in Kansas in 1874, **(The United States V. The Leavenworth, Lawrence & Galveston Railroad Company and The United States Of America V. The Missouri, Kansas And Texas Railway Company)** and was finally won in the United States Supreme Court in 1876 **(Leavenworth Lawrence and Galveston Railroad Company V. United States (92 U.S. 733) And Missouri Kansas and Texas Railway Company V. United States (1875) (92 U.S. 760))**. The two railroad corporations lost the appeal of their earlier defeat in 1874. In the meantime both companies had went into receivership and for years after the legal battle was over the settlers would have difficulty arranging payment for their attorneys.

Chapter 5: Comes the MK&T

By the fall of 1870, Ladore was as high as it was ever going to be. Its reputation was still somewhat the "wild" town, but as reported in the papers, the local citizenry after the lynching in May had largely retaken control of the town and area and the liquor problem was largely a thing of the past. It was pursuing the junction between the M.K.&T. division lines as the company built its way down toward the southern border of Kansas. At the same time it had become the geographical and political center for the upcoming legal battle over the land issue in Neosho and Labette counties. However, by the end of the year, Ladore would have essentially fallen, almost all of its citizens moving elsewhere and almost all of its buildings on the road south to a new town, Parsons.

The M.K.&T. track construction arrived at Ladore at just about the same time as the events of the Ladore Tragedy in May, 1870. This chapter will trace through the articles as the M.K.&T. was reaching Ladore and after as Ladore tried to become the junction of the M.K.&T. divisions coming down from Junction City, KS and Sedalia, MO. The tale of the ending of Ladore as an organized town revolves around its losing out on its efforts to be the junction of the M.K.&T. lines, and thus also the site for the major shop facilities, roundhouse, depot and offices of the company. These all were awarded to a new town just five miles down the line, Parsons. The tale has two versions. In one Ladore's greed robbed it of its chance. In the other the M.K.&T. manipulated events to set up its own town on its own terms. Both tales will be explored.

The M.K.&T. Reaches Ladore

As was mentioned earlier, through the month of April, 1870, there was an influx of people, both desirable and not so desirable in

Ladore. The citizens had been informed that Ladore would be a station point on the M.K.&T. after it arrived at Ladore. Bonds had been issued for the construction of the new schoolhouse. Forty acres of land had been donated and $2,000 subscribed for the building of a Catholic church [**N8. Osage Mission _Journal_, March 5, 1870, N14. Fort Scott _Monitor_, April 6-7, 1870**]. The Fort Scott _Monitor_ also reported in a short notice on April 20, 1870 that the M.K.&T. anticipated reaching Ladore within two weeks (15 days), thus putting the arrival of the "Katy" tracks in the first week of May.

The Osage Mission _Journal_ announced the first arrival of an M.K.&T. passenger train at Ladore as occurring on May 21, 1870 in its May 26th edition. In the last known Wheeler column in the Lawrence _Daily Republican Journal_, dated June 3, 1870, the columnist comments on the character of the people of Ladore and the effect of the publicity on the names of Fort Roach / Ladore based on the events of the previous month and the "end of the tracks" element:

--"God has sent us a better class of citizens than a new country is usally blessed with. In the town of Ladore, and in the country round about, we have people, young and old, who would grace the _best_ society anywhere. Our people are a reading people—a literary people. It takes a four-horse coach to carry their mails; and still the Government has provided us with no mail route. We have a large and well-conducted Sunday school, with as good a corps of officers and teachers as can be found anywhere. The Catholics, Presbyterians, Baptists, and Methodists (named in the order of organization) have organized church societies, and some of them are moving toward the erection of respectable church edifices. We have ministers, college-bred and theologically trained, who are fully capable of filling any pulpit in Lawrence or Chicago. And still strangers come here armed to the teeth, and carrying forty rounds of cartridges.."

-Lawrence *Daily Republican Journal,* June 3, 1870, "Letter from Neosho County"

Clearly Wheeler was making a plea to the posterity of the place for people to look beyond the short timers who were following the tracks and look deeper at the character of the people who had been trying to make of the place a good town for almost three years. To what degree its reputation, as exemplified in the poem "The Fall of Ladore," remained an albatross about the town's neck and its future ambitions is not certain. In the tales of Ladore's demise, neither version cites its wild reputation specifically, though the version placing the most blame on the town and not the company for Ladore's demise does seem to connect the dots between its being a den of vice and iniquity to its supposed greed in dealing with the M.K.&T. The Kansas *Daily Tribune* in its article discussing and advertising the upcoming 4th of July mass meeting at Ladore did its part to fire back a bit at the poem with the following little poetic blurb as it called upon the people of southern Kansas to show up at Ladore for the meeting:

> "All at once, and all o'er, with a mighty uproar,
> And this way the people turn out at Ladore."

- Daily Kansas *Tribune* (Lawrence), June 14, 1870, "The Gathering at Ladore"

The Osage Mission *Journal* also posted an article as to the changes in Ladore in an effort to try to help clean up the town's reputation.

--"We are pleased to learn that the better class of citizens at Ladore, understanding well the inciting cause that led to the late, deplorable tragedy in their midst, have determined that the law shall be executed restraining and regulating the sale of intoxicating liquors and that some regard shall be had for the observance of that 'higher law,' greater than all human enactments, which has declared that good order, sobriety, safety to life, limb, and honor, are [of] infinitely greater importance to any community than pandering for filthy lucre's sake to their debased tastes and passions of those who, unfortunately for themselves, are slaves to strong drink."

-Osage Mission *Journal*, June 22, 1870, "Law and Order at Ladore"

It should be noted that many leading citizens of Osage Mission were invested in Ladore, even to the point of having business interests in both locations and some citizens of Osage Mission being stockholders in the town company at Ladore. The bad publicity the town had received, like all bad publicity, can paint those around it with a broad brush, so it would be of everyone's interest for Ladore to be cleaning up itself, and for those communities around it to be publicizing that fact as well.

At the same time, the leaders of Ladore were not ignoring the future of the town and the role that the railroads could play. In the same June 22nd edition, the Osage Mission Journal also published this news item.

--"On Tuesday, Capt. Neely, Dr. Gabriel and John Hall, Esq. of Ladore, were in the city looking after the railroad interests of their town. Ladore is wide-awake and is making a strong effort to become a railroad center."

-Osage Mission *Journal*, June 22, 1870

And further on the vein of Ladore becoming a center of communication and travel connection in southern Neosho County, the *Journal* published this item as well on June 30th.

--"Today Tisdale & Co. commence running a good coach daily between this place [Osage Mission] and Ladore, reaching here at 9 a.m. and leaving at 3 p.m. connecting with the 5 o'clock Northern train. Fare is $1.50 each way or $2.50 for the round trip."

Osage Mission *Journal*, June 30, 1870, "New Stage Line"

To further see the efforts of Ladore in terms of securing the junction, consider the items from two articles posted on July 22nd and 23rd, respectively in the Neosho County *Dispatch* and the Fort Scott *Monitor*:

--"The townships of Mission and Ladore are to vote on the 16th of next month on the respective propositions to take stock to the amount of $80,000 and $25,000 in the Tebo and Neosho Railroad, (Sedalia and Fort Scott) and to issue bonds therefore, provided the company shall build said road through the towns of Mission and Ladore within one year from the above date."

- Neosho County *Dispatch*, July 22, 1870

--"Ladore is a beautiful site for a town, and claims to be the place where will be formed the junction of the Sedalia and Fort Scott road with the Missouri, Kansas and Texas road, and the indications are that it stands a very good chance of securing it. Three townships in Neosho have taken steps toward bonding aid of the building of the road, and there is no prospect of any other locality contesting the field. This secured, and Ladore stock will be up in the market."

--"The railroad company recently had three hundred and sixty acres of its ground laid off into lots, and the wise ones hereabouts think 'that means *something*.'"

Fort Scott *Monitor*, July 23, 1870, "Letter from Ladore"

These items from the two papers certainly indicate Ladore recognized its vested interested in obtaining the junction and that there was a push to try to enact bonded debt to get it. The second quoted item from the *Monitor*, as well as other passaged that occurred in columns and articles in 1870 will bear noticing in considering the two versions of the tale of Ladore's demise. Picking up on the topic, the Osage Mission *Journal* published two notices on July 28th of particular note:

--"Railroad Depot. – We understand the M.K.&T. R.R. have built a fine Depot at Ladore, said to be one of the best on the entire line."

--"Also that that Co. have laid out an extensive addition to the town site, which betokens 'large expectations' for that enterprising place. We rejoice in these evidences of her future prosperity."

Osage Mission *Journal*, July 28, 1870

Again mark the second item quoted from the *Journal* on July 28th for inspection later.

Then on August 4th, the Osage Mission Journal also repeated its items it published on the 28th of July. And not to be outdone, in another item published in the Fort Scott *Monitor* on July 31st, the following was stated.

--"There are several business houses in Ladore, and the town seems to be prospering. The railroad company has recently built a very good depot at this place, and the business community now enjoy all the privileges of the M.K.&T. Railroad. Ladore has submitted the proposition of voting $25,000 in township bonds to the railroad from Fort Scott, and strong hopes are entertained by the citizens that this will secure the junction of the two roads."

Fort Scott *Monitor*, July 31, 1870, "A Trip to the Country"

Based on what was passing as "common" knowledge during the summer of 1870, the papers and the towns of southeast Kansas seemed prepared to "make book" on the prospect of Ladore being the junction of the two M.K.&T. divisions and the main town on the line in Kansas. The Osage Mission *Journal* also announced the opening of an express office in Ladore on August 25th. Things seemed to be running all Ladore's way. In further emphasis of this point, and to fully realize the extent that the publicity was being let out that Ladore would be "the" place, a column profiling the current situation in Ladore, published in the Osage Mission Journal on September 1st, must be considered. This particular column is so full of information that it will be included in its entirety, with one part in particular emphasized for later consideration.

--"EDITOR'S JOURNAL:-- As Ladore expects to be the terminus (for some time, at least) of the T.&N. R.R. and the point at which that road forms a junction with the M.K.&T. R.R., a few facts relating to our town and country, would probably be interesting to your readers.

Ladore was laid off by the M.K.&T. R.R. Co., in the month of May last and is situated near the center of the county east and west, and on the southern tier of Townships being about 30 miles from Humboldt, 20 miles from New Chicago, and 12 miles from Osage Mission, containing at present about eighty houses among which are four Hotels, two feed and Livery Stables, two Blacksmith shops, two Carpenter shops, five Dry good stores, one Hardware and tin shop, one Book and stationery store, several family groceries, one Whiskey shop, one Drug store, one Millinery shop, one Boot and Shoe shop, with the usual number of Doctor and Law shops, a good District school house, here too the M.K.&T. R.R. Co. have a fine depot; the enterprising firm of Hall Brothers are making and have made the best quality of brick we have seen in the State. Adjoining the town site is the famous "Blue Limestone quarry" which extends over acres of land, is near the surface being easily quarried, and in layers of from three inches thick to that of three feet thick, in color dark blue and very solid, and when placed in buildings is beautiful and substantial. There is an abundance of it there to build a city. The country surrounding Ladore, comprises the valleys of Big and Little Labette creeks, and Chetopa creeks, is as beautiful, fertile, well watered and timbered as any in the county or Southern Kansas. The high prairie lands are fertile, rolling but not broken, and on these lands the farmers are this year blessed with abundant crops "and peace plenty" and our babies sit smiling at the door."

-Osage Mission *Journal*, September 1, 1870, "From Ladore"

Even from the Wheeler columns earlier in the year, the extent of Ladore's growth is shown in this article. From needing a hotel earlier in the year, by September there were four of them. Wheeler put the count earlier in the year at three dry goods and general merchandise houses, one butcher shop and meat market, a boot and shoe maker, a blacksmith shop, a stove and hardware store and two doctors. Based on the September 1st article in the *Journal*, two livery stables, one blacksmith shop, two carpenter shops, two more dry goods stores, a stationary store, several groceries, a whisky shop, a drug store and law firms (T.C. Cory, for example) had been added. Quarrying activity was taking place and there was a firm on site making bricks for building that was not noted as being present before. Thus, from the arrival of the M.K.&T. to September, the town was booming in anticipation of being the junction point on the M.K.&T. system.

There are excerpts from a few more articles published in October of 1870 that are pertinent to setting the stage for the comparison of the stories of Ladore's demise. The first, published in the Fort Scott *Monitor* on October 11th, reads as follows:

--"It is now pretty generally conceded that Ladore will be the place of the junction of the M.K.&T. R.R. and the Sedalia and Fort Scott road. Neosho [County] will have as many miles of railroad in the county as most any other county in the State."

Fort Scott *Monitor*, October 11, 1870

Almost as a response to the *Monitor* article, although it was printed three days before it, is the following article in its entirety from the New Chicago *Transcript*.

--"Lots at the town of Ladore were thrown into market during this week. We learn that good prices were obtained for those that were sold, we presume under the impression that Ladore is to be the Junction of the Sedalia branch of the M.K.&T. Railway with the main line. *While it would give us great pleasure to record the fact that our county is to receive the Junction, and that by said connection a live, prosperous town would be built up, yet from present indications and judging from what we have learned from very good authority, we are afraid that we shall not be called upon to make such announcement. 'Lay not the flattering unction to your souls," gentlemen, that Ladore is to be the Junction; if you do you are likely to be disappointed.'"*

- New Chicago *Transcript*, October 8, 1870, "Lots for Sale"

So, publicly at least, the lots the M.K.&T. had laid out were now open for sale and buyers were coming in. The *Transcript*, however, had seemed to smell something on the wind that the other papers were not getting. The *Transcript* would prove to be correct by the end of the year, in fact, almost literally within the month. The following item from the *Tribune* was picked up by the Osage Mission *Journal* and published on November 10th.

--"A correspondent of the State *Tribune* writes up the new town of Parsons as follows:

PARSONS, LABETTE CO., Oct. 31.

EDITOR TRIBUNE: Having just received orders from headquarters to commence work at this place, which is the point of junction of the Sedalia division with the Kansas division of the Missouri, Kansas & Texas railway, I deem it of great importance to the people of Lawrence to know of its location as a business point."

Osage Mission *Journal*, November 10, 1870, "Parsons"

At this point the stage is set for the third act of the play. The "villain" has made its appearance, if there is a villain to this piece. All that remains is to decide which version of the story needs not just to be told, but to be remembered.

Chapter 6: Founding of Parsons / Ladore on Sleds

The most told version of the story when speaking to citizens of Parsons who remember hearing about Ladore is the "greedy citizen" version, which is the version that will be found in most of the printed historical sources that can be found that mention Ladore, albeit very briefly. Both versions are remembered in one form or another in an article published in the Chanute *Tribune* of June 13, 1912.

Version I:

--"'The reason Ladore died was because it tried to hold up the railroad company,' said an old settler this morning.

'The company wanted to build its roundhouse and establish quarters there. Ladore insisted on charging a fabulous price for the site sought, so the railroad company went to Parsons, where it had been offered a site free of charge and adjoining land at reasonable rates.'

'There was a Ladore before there was a Parsons, but after the railroad company made Parsons its headquarters, Ladore languished and finally became no more.'"

Version II:

--"'This statement is true with some exceptions," said another pioneer. "There was never any intention on the part of the Katy railroad of forming a junction of its Sedalia and Junction City lines at Ladore and establishing roundhouses and machine shops there. The original plan of the Katy was to form the junction at Chetopa, and the first railroad map of the road had Chetopa down on it in big letters, and the map can be produced if necessary.'

'He [Robert S. Stevens] changed the plans of the company as to the junction of the two lines, and he, with other men of the railroad, organized the Parsons Town Company and made the junction there.'"

- Chanute *Tribune*, June 13, 1912, "Another Reason Why Ladore Fell"

Analysis of Version I:

What is the evidence for or against the first version of the demise of Ladore? On the "for" side would have been some published story about such a dispute in the newspapers at the time. But to date, nothing of the sort has been found. The accounts that have been found that tell the story of a land price dispute between the citizens of Ladore and the M.K.&T. are, like the article source above, printed or told years, if not decades, after the fact. One source is W.W. Graves' *History of Neosho County*, which was put together many years after the events at Ladore and quotes William G. Cutler's *History of the State of Kansas* which was published in 1883:

--But the avaricious action of the owners of the land, was the secret of its overthrow, for no sooner had the site of Parsons become fixed, than the city, now called Ladore, was wholly moved to that place, and nothing remains of Ladore but a railroad side track, a farm residence, a church building and the post office.

- Cutler, William G., *History of the State of Kansas*, A. T. Andreas, Chicago, IL, 1883.

However, while there was a price dispute that is part of the historical record involving settlers and the M.K.&T., it involves settlers around the Parsons town site, not Ladore. As stated in the *History of Parsons*: 1869-1895, then followed up in the book by V.V. Masterson, *The Katy Railroad and the Last Frontier*", the story goes as follows.

Sometime in October of 1870, the Parsons Town Company was organized by Robert S. Stevens. Masterson puts the date at October 17, and the Parsons History book states the charter for the company was filed with the Kansas Secretary of State on October 24, 1870. The officers of the company were Isaac Goodnow, N.S. Goss, F.C. White, O.B. Gunn, Norman Eastman and Robert S. Stevens. Most of these worthies, if not all, were M.K.&T. men. There will be several items to be quoted in relation to this when considering the second version of the story, but what is pertinent to the analysis of the first version is the following:

--"The town having been located, the company soon encountered difficulties in acquiring title to as large a body of land as they hoped to secure, and we may readily believe that it was for the purpose of influencing these parties to make terms that the action of the town company—an account of which is given below — was taken, rather than with any serious intention of carrying out the determination therein expressed, for no steps were taken looking to an abandonment of the site which had been selected and partly surveyed; but for some purpose, probably by the company's direction, certain resolutions by it adopted were published in several papers, and more or less was said through the press on "Parsons defunct."

- History of Parsons, 1869-1895, **page 6**

The press notice mentioned in the quote was published in papers across southern Kansas in December of 1870, the action taken to get the previous settlers around the area where the Parsons Town Company wanted to establish their town to either vacate or sell their claims at what the M.K.&T. viewed as a more reasonable price. The notice was published in such papers as the Humboldt *Union*, the New Chicago *Transcript*, the Osage Mission *Journal*, the *Daily* Tribune of Lawrence, the Fort Scott *Monitor* and the Oswego *Register*. The notice was dated December 22, 1870 and published in the papers some time during the last week of December that year.

--"NEOSHO FALLS, Kan., Dec. 22, 1870

Eds. *Union*: -- Inclosed you have resolutions passed by the Directors of the Parsons Town Company, and confirmed by the president of the M.K.&T. Co. You will see that the present town site of Parsons is abandoned, as the orders are to erect not even a station house there. If you think these facts are of sufficient interest to your readers you are at liberty to publish the accompanying resolutions. Very Respectfully,

I.T. Goodnow

At a meeting of the Board of Directors of the Parsons Town Company, held at Sedalia, Mo., on the 14th inst. the following resolutions were unanimously adopted:

WHEREAS, The Missouri, Kansas & Texas Railway Company having decided to locate its machine shops and other important buildings elsewhere than at the junction of its Sedalia and Neosho divisions, thus rendering the building up of any large town at the junction impracticable:

[Resolved, that the] Board of Directors of the Parsons Town Company hereby abandon all idea of locating or building a town on sections 18 or 19 in town 31, of range 19, east, or anywhere in the vicinity; the decision of said railway company above referred to rendering such action necessary.

Resolved. That the treasurer of said town company is hereby directed to sell all lands intended for town site purposes, at such price as he may deem fit and proper at the earliest day practicable.

R.S. Stevens, Pres.
John. R. Wheat, Sec'y"

- Osage Mission *Journal*, December 29, 1870, "Parsons Abandoned"

It is quite possible that, years or decades after the fact, the people were remembering the wrong event in terms of a price dispute.

There was even a similar dispute that occurred between the M.K.&T. and the city of Fort Scott earlier in 1870. Fort Scott was also a candidate for the machine shop and roundhouse facilities that the M.K.&T. was planning to locate near the center of its envisioned rail system. As reported in the Parsons *Sun* in 1921:

--"This history is that Fort Scott had a contract for the shops and that land owners boosted the price of the available real estate. The railroad officials are said to have gone to the Fort Scott council with a request to be permitted to erect the shops outside the city limits—in order to evade the excessive prices. Permission being granted, the shops were immediately located in Parsons."

- Parsons *Sun*, March 7, 1921, Parsons 50th Anniversary Edition

In Masterson's book, the original area the M.K.&T. was to receive from the city of Fort Scott was not of sufficient size to build the facilities there. An alternate area was found, and the price demanded by the owner in that area was set at $1,000 per acre. In response, according to Masterson, Stevens chose to back out of the deal with Fort Scott because of the land "muddle" created by the Fort Scott city government and chose his own location farther south (the new town of Parsons),[Masterson, page 82]. The Fort Scott *Monitor* in 1870 and 1871 also mentioned the failure of the M.K.&T. to build the roundhouse, depot and machine shops as contracted.

--"The Board of County Commissioners of Bourbon county met yesterday, and closed the contract for the completion of the Tebo & Neosho (M.K.&T. R.R.) to Ft. Scott by the first of January, 1871."

--"Here the line leads out to the southwest to connect with the Junction City branch at some point in the Neosho Valley, which will give Fort Scott connection with that rich and fertile valley."

--"The Missouri, Kansas & Texas railway also has entered into a contract with the city of Ft. Scott to make it the end of an operating division, and to build their machine shops at this place..."

- Fort Scott *Monitor*, July 3, 1870, "The Contract Closed"

Three days later, on July 6th, the *Monitor* published an article updating the status of the contract with the M.K.&T. By that time the local officials in Bourbon County and Ft. Scott had signed their contracts, and Dr. Hepler had begun a trip to Sedalia to meet with Robert S. Stevens and have the contract signed by the railroad company. In a letter dated July 2nd, as reported in the *Monitor* article of the 6th of July, Robert Stevens stated the following:

--"As to the apprehension that the depots and machine shops may be located too far from the business portions of the city, he says: 'Rest assured it never has been our practice, and shall not be in your case, to disturb or derange business relations, nor to build up rival towns, especially when people act in the liberal spirit of your citizens."

- Fort Scott *Monitor*, July 6, 1870, "The Exact Status"

This passage in the *Monitor* seems to parallel with the statement in Masterson's book that the M.K.&T. had chosen to change location relative to the location in Fort Scott. It does seem to imply that there was concern in Fort Scott by July of 1870 that the M.K.&T. facilities would be located too far from the business interests of the city. By July 17th, the *Monitor* published an ordinance voted by the city council of Fort Scott for purpose of holding a bond election to help finance the construction of the M.K.&T. road through Fort Scott and the subsequent construction of round house, machine shops, etc. The ordinance called for a special election to vote for approval of the bonds. The bonds were to be for the amount of $75,000, earning 7% interest, and payable to the railroads in 30 years. The agreement also allowed for the issuing of a further

$25,000 in bonds, or rather than issuing the bonds, the city would purchase the right of way through Fort Scott for the railroad company, and an additional 20 acres besides for no more than $15,000. The additional land would be ground for the construction of the shops and roundhouse. The stipulation for the company was that the line through Fort Scott would be considered the main line of the road, that Fort Scott would be the end of a division, that the freight facilities, machine shops, depots, roundhouses, etc. would be built on the purchased land (or land purchased by the railroad using the $25,000 additional bonds), and that no such facilities would be build south and west of Fort Scott on the M.K.&T. system until first the facilities at Fort Scott were completed.

The ordinance further stipulated that the special election would be held on August 22nd, 1870; but this date was changed and the election held on August 30th, the election notice setting the date being published on August 25th. The reported vote in the *Monitor* on August 31st, totaling from all three wards, was 523 for the bond agreement versus 3 against. By October, 1870 the Parsons Town Company was formed and any possibility of shops, etc. at Fort Scott was abandoned by the M.K.&T. By September, 1871 the city of Parsons had been established, most of Ladore's buildings had been moved down to the new town, and the citizens of Fort Scott were calling for a repudiation of the bonds they had voted for the previous year on the basis of breach of contract. The full particulars of the contract of July 30th, 1870 were reprinted in the *Monitor* on September 19, 1871.

So, while there was plenty in the press with respect to land price disputes and problems with Fort Scott and the settlers in the area of the not as yet established city of Parsons in 1870, there has been nothing found reported as to a dispute with the settlers at Ladore, except in memories long after the fact. While this is not definitive, it is buttressed by several points about the town site of Ladore that were, in fact, published at the time and give evidence against the first version of the story.

Item: In 1869 there was a Kinman Town Company formed **[KS Secretary of State Records]** formed at or near the town site which later in 1869 was changed to the Ladore Town Company. So there was a town company in place, ran out of Osage Mission, before the arrival of the M.K.&T. What makes this significant is the further statements regarding the plats filed on the town site of Ladore.

Item: Wheeler mentioned in his column to the Lawrence *Journal* on March 8, 1870: **"town site on railroad land."**

Item: From the Ft. Scott *Monitor*, July 23, 1870: **"The railroad company recently had three hundred and sixty acres of its ground laid off into lots, and the wise ones hereabouts think 'that means something.'"**

Item: From the Osage Mission *Journal*, July 28, 1870: **"Also that that Co. have laid out an extensive addition to the town site,"**

Item: From the Osage Mission *Journal*, September 1, 1870: **"Ladore was laid off by the M.K.&T. R.R. Co., in the month of May last"**

Item: The official plat map of the Ladore town site, filed in the Register of Deeds Office in the Neosho County Courthouse, and the only one on file, shows the line of the M.K.&T. R.R. and the location of the depot. This is probably the plat map filed by the M.K.&T.

Item: The Chanute *Times* on August 7, 1875 posted a "Notice of Sale of Land for the Delinquent Taxes of the Year 1874." In this notice was listed, in table form, Ladore City. The summary is as follows and consists of all the lots on the town site: Blocks 1-62, Lots 1-12 in each block; Blocks 63-70, Lots 1-14 in each block. The named owner of all of the Ladore City town site was the M.K.&T. Railway Co.

From the preponderence of evidence it seems clear that there would not have been a price dispute on the town site where the M.K.&T. was thinking about setting up shop, when the M.K.&T. owned the land in question already. The land records show J.N. Roach was located south of 20th road on the south edge of the platted town site. The school was and cemetery is located one half mile north of 20th road, along what is marked as 25th road on the county maps. It is possible that the land of the old Kinman/Ladore Town Co. might have been located south of 20th road between Lyon and Meade roads. The state records show Ladore as being located in Section 27, Township 30 S, Range 19 E. They also list the location of Kinman as the SE ¼ of Section 27, Township 30 S, Range 19 E. There is a hand-written annotation on the record for Kinman that notes the location as being ½ mile south in section 34 of the same Township 30 S and Range 19 E. It is possible that the M.K.&T. might have wanted to induce the settlers already present to move south onto the platted land the M.K.&T. itself owned, and sell to the company the land on the old town site in order to build shops, roundhouse, etc. on that land. It is possible, but the overall evidence, especially evidence supporting the second version of Ladore's demise, makes this seem unlikely.

The two images below are drawn from "The Official State Atlas of Kansas", L.H. Everts & Co., Philadelphia, 1887 **[B9. Historic Atlas of Kansas Counties]**. The first image is a full view of the

Township of Ladore in southern Neosho County, Kansas. The second is an expanded view of sections 27 and 34 of Township 30 S, Range 19 E, showing the official locations of Ladore and Kinman as stated in the state records. The road at the boundary between Sections 27 and 34 is 20th road today. The land records at the Neosho County Courthouse in Erie, Kansas list the northernmost sections in section 34 as originally being owned by J.N. Roach.

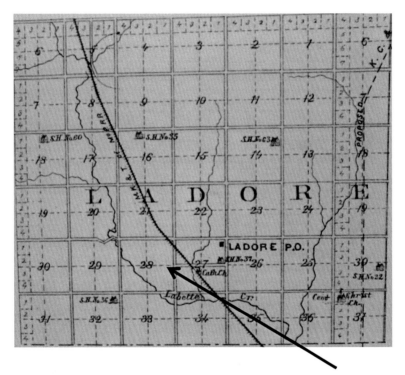

Ladore Township, Neosho County, Kansas: note that 25th Road in this 1887 atlas map is shown completely dividing Section 27. The Ladore school is shown at the intersection of 25th Road and Meade Road. The Catholic Church at Ladore is shown just about where the Ladore Cemetery stands today. The town site map on file shows the town occupying the two southern quarter sections of Section 27.

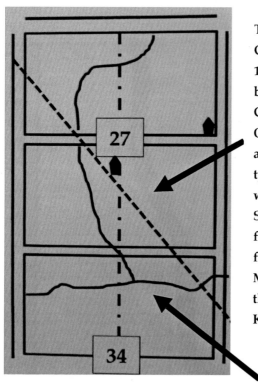

The Kinman Town Charter, filed July 28, 1869, and incorporated by D.R. Kinman, R.D. Cogswell, John O'Grady, A.F. Neely, and John Ryan. The typed record indicates it was in the SE ¼ of Section 27. The founders were town fathers of Osage Mission at the time of the founding of the Kinman Co.

The hand written annotation found on the microfilm record from the Kansas Historical Society notes the location of Kinman as incorporated as further south in Section 34. Moses McKinley (M.M.) Neely is listed as the postmaster in each document for 1870-71.

Analysis of Version II:

V.V. Masterson's book, *The Katy Railroad and the Last Frontier* and the book *Parsons History: 1869-1895* have the most to say with regard to the M.K.&T.'s intentions through the year 1870 with regard to forming the junction of their two divisions and then building on toward the southern state line. The company was in a race with the L.L.&G. railroad and the Kansas City, Fort Scott & Gulf (the "Border Tier") railroad for the southern state line of Kansas. The winner would receive exclusive right to enter the Indian Territory and build through to the markets of Texas and an additional land grant through the Indian Territory on either side of the proposed line of the road.

The second version, in more detail, goes along like this. Ladore was never really in the running for the junction point of the Sedalia and Neosho divisions of the M.K.&T. According to the old pioneer in the Chanute *Tribune* account of June 1912, the original junction point was to be Chetopa, just a few miles from the southern boundary of the state. According to the article some proposed land deals fell through in Chetopa and caused Robert Stevens to change plans as to the junction point. By the end of the year, 1870, it was planned for the M.K.&T. road to reach the state line. The junction point would be somewhere along that line.

A station called Dayton, about 10 miles south of Ladore and located where the railroad would bend southeast toward Oswego and Chetopa, was established on the line after the M.K.&T. had built through Ladore. Dayton was located a few miles northwest of Labette City. According to Masterson, a game was to be played by the M.K.&T. using Ladore and Dayton as public targets for the location of the junction, all the while the company would be buying land and setting up its own town midway between the two locations. This became the city of Parsons.

For evidence of the Ladore-Dayton "gambit" it is necessary to bring in some of the backstory as to the M.K.&T. Railroad Co., Ladore, and the birth of Parsons as told in Masterson's book. The source for this is "The Katy Railroad and the Last Frontier," by V.V. Masterson. The pertinent details are shown below **[B7. Masterson]**.

- **Page 51** – In March, 1870, Robert S. Stevens, general manager of the M.K.&T. traveling with Major Otis Gunn, chief engineer of the M.K.&T. and John Scullin, chief foreman of construction, visited Ladore, then traveled south and picked the spot for the future town of Parsons.

- **Page 62** – In late May or early June, 1870, Stevens orders Gunn to put a sign up for Dayton at mile marker 160. Ladore was atmile marker 150, and the railhead had just reached the midpointbetween, where Parsons was to be placed. The goal, Masterson claims, was to shift focus to the two stations, Ladore and Dayton, as possible points for the junction of the Sedalia and Junction City lines while the true point, Parsons, was to be established, the Town Co. being formed and dominated by the M.K.&T.

- **Page 88** – Robert S. Stevens organized the Parsons Town Company on October 17, 1870.

- **Page 84** – November 7 & 8, 1870, ground is broken by the MKT construction gangs for the town of Parsons and the rail junction of the two M.K.&T. lines.

In addition to these points in the Masterson book. Wheeler verifies Stevens' presence in Ladore in February to March of 1870 in his letter of February 25th, published in the Lawrence *Journal* on March 8th. Saying **"R.S. Stevens is in town tonight, and says the cars will be running through here by the first of May."**

On the timing of the establishment of Dayton as a town on the M.K.&T. line, a notice in the Fort Scott *Monitor*, published early in June, fixes the establishment of Dayton in late May or in the first week of June and gives some detail as to the early development of the place.

--**"A new town called Dayton is located on the M.K.&T. railroad, about ten miles from Oswego. It is in the midst of a rich country with plenty** of wood, coal and water convenient. It has already a grist mill and blacksmith shop, and several dry goods and grocery stores will be opened as soon as the buildings can be erected."

- Fort Scott *Monitor*, June 5, 1870, "Items from Southern Kansas"

The Parsons History book, put together by the Parsons Public Library and drawing from articles in the *Sun*, the *Eclipse* and the *Republican* newspapers in Parsons, Nelson Cases' history of Labette County and the *Memorial and Historical Magazine* of Mrs. Augustus Wilson, also puts the formation of the Parsons Town Co. as occurring on October 17th and has its charter filed formally on October 24th in Topeka. As shown earlier, it lists the original charter members of the company, most of whom, if not all, were M.K.&T. officials.

A small community named Mendota had been established in the area where the M.K.&T. was looking to establish Parsons. The Parsons History book names the following settlers as living on the land of interest to the M.K.&T.: John Leonard, W.K. Hayes, Abraham Fults, John Kendall, Aaron Midkiff, John Davis, Abraham Cary, Mr. Simpson, Anson Kellogg, S. Eves, Henry Baker, H.L. Partridge, and George Briggs [History of Parsons – pages 2-3]. The following statement is also pertinent in terms of the land price dispute that occurred over the site of Parsons:

--"Several of these parties were unwilling to dispose of their interests, and negotiations to secure title were in progress for some time."

- History of Parsons: 1869-1895, page 3

The Parsons History book also notes that L.F. Olney, civil engineer for the M.K.&T., arrived at the Parsons town site on October 26th to begin laying off the town site. It also states that C.G. Wait, another engineer for the road, located the junction point formally on November 6th, and then the contractors broke dirt at the junction point two days later.

The Parsons History book further notes this on the Parsons Town Co.:

--"The company was formed expressly for the purpose of laying off and building a railroad town. It was believed that the junction of the two branches of the M. K. & T. was the most feasible point for the location of a town, where would almost certainly be located the machine shops and offices."

--"Of course these parties knew the point where this junction must be made before their incorporation, for not only was section 19 designated in the charter as the central point, but their surveyor was on the ground before the railroad engineer had actually designated the connecting point."

- History of Parsons: 1869-1895, page 5

Now, turning back to the record as given by the newspaper articles of the time with regard to this matter. The passage printed in the New Chicago *Transcript* seems prescient and the entire article needs to be examined in light of the information so far uncovered regarding the apparent publicly known future of Ladore:

--"Lots at the town of Ladore were thrown into market during this week. We learn that good prices were obtained for those that were sold, we presume under the impression that Ladore is to be the Junction of the Sedalia branch of the M.K.&T. Railway with the main line. While it would give us great pleasure to record the fact that our county is to receive the Junction, and that by said connection a live, prosperous town would be built up, *yet from present indications and judging from what we have learned from very good authority, we are afraid that we shall not be called upon to make such announcement. "Lay not the flattering unction to your souls," gentlemen, that Ladore is to be the Junction; if you do you are likely to be disappointed.*"

- New Chicago *Transcript*, October 8, 1870, "Lots for Sale"

According to the timeline so far established, the company had planned to make a location south of Ladore the junction point as early as the spring of 1870. The date of incorporation of the Parsons Town Co. is stated as October 17th, with its papers being filed in Topeka a week later. It is reasonable to assume that discussion of forming the company and hashing out the language for its charter would have occurred some time before the 17th. With this in mind, the article in the *Transcript* of the 8th then shows potentially two things.

First, given that the company had laid out their own plat map of Ladore, it was then content to throw the lots onto the market "under the impression that Ladore is to be the junction of the Sedalia branch … with the main line." Why open the lots in Ladore for sale? Perhaps the company wanted speculators to focus on and purchase land at Ladore, gaining income from the sales, and at the same time insure that it was not disturbed in its plans for Parsons.

Secondly, unless Crowther, the editor of the *Transcript* was very good at reading the future, it seems that someone at the M.K.&T. may have let the secret slip a bit. The *Transcript* was published in New Chicago, at the junction of the L.L.&G. and the M.K.&T. in the northwest corner of Neosho County. It was a supporter and platted out along the M.K.&T. line on the east side of what would become Chanute. It is possible that Crowther at least heard some discussion, if not being outright told, of what the M.K.&T. was doing in the southern part of the county.

A further notice as to the fate of both Ladore and Parsons was printed in the Fort Scott *Monitor* just after the Parsons Town Company was formed on October 17th.

--"We learn from a reliable source that the junction of the Missouri, Kansas & Texas and Sedalia & Fort Scott road will be at a point five or six miles south of Ladore, in Labette county. A town is to be laid off at the junction, and will be christened Parsons, in honor of the President of the two roads."

As far as Fort Scott was concerned in October, 1870 it had a contract with the M.K.&T. in place, and a bond election just recently held to secure the financing for construction of the line, the shops and the other M.K.&T. facilities therein. The penny had not yet dropped for the people in Fort Scott with respect to the notice that the junction of the lines would be at a new town, Parsons, south of Ladore in Neosho County.

The game was fully up for all concerned by November 10th when the Osage Mission *Journal* published a profile of the birthing of the town of Parsons, and stated openly in the article that the company was intending on making Parsons the junction point, as well as the site of construction for the machine shops, the roundhouse and a major depot station. The Parsons History book notes on its third page that by November 11th, John Austin had moved a house down from Ladore and located it on the Parsons town site. The house was located on the northwest corner of what is now the junction of Central and Crawford avenues, directly north of where the police station is located. A mini-strip mall occupies the block today. Parsons acted like a magnet, drawing in buildings and businesses from Dayton, from Labette City and other local settlements as well as Ladore. The count, based on the Parsons History book is that there were from 50 to 75 houses and buildings moved from Ladore to Parsons over the winter of 1870-71 [B5. **History of Parsons, page 10**].

From the comparison of record to story, it seems that the second version of the story of the end of Ladore is the more likely. More evidence as to a land price dispute seems to come from a dispute over land in Fort Scott and on the nascent Parsons town site as there were settlers already occupying land that the company wanted to use for the town. In Ladore, while there had been a settlement there for nearly three years, the company platted out its own site instead and was the owner of record when the town site was sold for tax delinquency years later. The evidence makes it is apparent that it was a business decision and some questionable tactics by the M.K.&T. that ultimately brought about the end of Ladore.

Evidence for the Dayton side of the story comes from an article published in the Labette *Sentinel* in January, 1871. The article as published shows that the editor, and by extension perhaps the people of Labette City, were under the impression that *they* were to be candidates for the junction of the two M.K.&T. lines. Labette City and Oswego were rivals for the Labette county seat at the time, and Thomas Irish, the editor of the *Sentinel*, put the existence of Dayton as an attempt by the leaders of Oswego and the M.K.&T. to injure the prospects of Labette City. The pertinent quotes are as follows:

--"Ever since the organization of the town of Labette, the people of Oswego have recognized in her a powerful and dangerous rival, and have not flinched to resort to any and every measure that would tend to dampen or blight her prospects. The first, the Dayton scheme, was a magnificent failure. Their bribery to defeat the junction of the Sedalia road at this place was *at that time* a partial success."

--"Their paid agents on the M.K.&T. R.R., to puff Oswego and lie about Labette, have injured their own town."

- Labette *Sentinel*, January 5, 1871, "Oswego's Last Struggle"

In the same issue of the *Sentinel*, in a profile of Labette City, the paper made the following statement of the situation at Parsons based on the notice published to "abandon" Parsons that was published in December, 1870 and early January, 1871. The paper referred to Parsons as **"this strictly railroad town to be run and ruled by corporations."** The report on the situation at Parsons and a further comment on Dayton were as follows:

--"Parsons is a myth. The squatters on section eighteen have twenty days to tear down their shanties, and remove their tents, and give the wolf again his hole and the rattlesnake their quarters."

--"She [Labette City] has lived to see Dayton, a town conceived at midnight in the barrooms of Oswego, and born a triplet on the trackless prairie, the protegee of the present county seat, 'wink out' unhonored, and unsung."

- Labette *Sentinel*, January 5, 1871, "Labette City"

As to the old timer's recollection of Chetopa as a target for the junction of the divisions of the M.K.&T., there has been no definitive article found to date. There is however, this notice, first published in the Chetopa *Advance* and then reprinted in the Lawrence *Journal* in November 1869, about a year before the M.K.&T. reached the southern border of Kansas.

--"A rousing railroad meeting was held at Spaulding's Hall on Saturday evening last. The meeting was large and enthusiastic. Hon. Levi Parsons, Mr. Dennison, and Col. N.S. Goss were present and addressed the meeting. A hearty welcome was extended to them by our citizens, and a disposition was manifested to use every reasonable exertion to secure for Chetopa the railroad advantages we have so earnestly looked for. – *Chetopa Advance*."

- Lawrence *Republican Journal*, November 6, 1869

It is likely that the railroad advantages discussed at this meeting were more that Chetopa would be on the M.K.&T. line and would, in effect, be the gateway for the railroad into the Indian Territory. A junction point for divisions was probably not a topic as the Tebo and Neosho line was not absorbed into the M.K.&T. as the Sedalia division until later in 1870.

So far as the record seems to recount, there was plenty of speculation in the region at the time as to the location of the junction point of the two divisions of the M.K.&T. and the consequent location of the freight, depot, roundhouse and machine shop facilities. At about the same point in 1870 the town of Fort Scott had contracted for them, Ladore was lobbying for and many papers in the region were thinking it would get them, Labette City thought it was in the running, Dayton was created and apparently promoted as a potential site as well. As to land price disputes, it was fairly well documented that Fort Scott and the settlers around the new town of Parsons had disagreements with the M.K.&T. and any mention of such a dispute with the people of Ladore does not appear in print until decades later. In the end the town of Ladore ended up an abandoned way station on the M.K.&T. line, and Parsons had the benefit of the largess of the M.K.&T.

Chapter 7: Ladore/Parsons

What Ladore brought to Parsons

The end of the story of Ladore in the 19th century as an incorporated town is a tale of buildings and people moving across Labette Creek and the fields from Neosho County to Labette County and resettling on the site of the new town of Parsons. In a very real sense Ladore was one of the seeds from which Parsons as the "Infant Wonder" and "Queen City of the Southwest" sprung. Many of the early standing buildings on the town site were buildings moved in whole; or disassembled and reassembled at Parsons. In addition, some of the prominent founding fathers of Parsons were former residents of Ladore. Men such as Dr. George Gabriel, the lawyer T.C. Cory, Capt. M.M. Neely, his brother Dr. A.F. Neely and Dr. C.B. Kennedy were men of influence in the founding of Parsons and helped to shape the town it would become. Perhaps the true legacy of Ladore is in the early life of Parsons. Parsons never experienced the "wild" days that Ladore did in anticipation of the railroad.

The following passages are drawn from the **"History of Parsons: 1869-1895"** with regard to business houses and other structures of note that were moved down from Ladore in late 1870 and early 1871.

--**"...in addition to two or three business houses which preceded it, on November 11, 1870, John Austin had on the ground the first dwelling put thereon** [the Parsons town site].**"**

- "History of Parsons: 1869-1895", page 3-4

The dwelling house described was placed on what is now the northeast corner Central and Crawford streets. Today that lot is occupied by a mini-mall that contains a laundromat on its eastern end and Chubby's Restaurant on its western end. It sits across the street north of where the Parsons Police Department is currently located. Austin's house was described as a two-story dwelling, and initially it was used for a boarding house.

The Parsons History book further adds the following details about the Austin house:

--"In front of this building the next spring he set out some maple trees, which were the first trees planted in the place. On these premises Dr. G.W. Gabriel has for many years had his home."

- "History of Parsons: 1869-1895", page 4

The quantity of houses and buildings moved from Ladore during the winter of 1870 to 1871 was estimated at from 50 to 75 in number. A significant contribution to a nascent town whose lots had not even officially come up for sale **[B5. History of Parsons, page 4]**. The Parsons History book also located or mentioned the following buildings from Ladore:

Page 11: Finus Smith tore down a 24 by 40 foot building and moved it to the northwest corner of Riggs (now Central) and Johnson (now Main) on the lot where the Commercial Bank now stands. He operated it as a hotel, and in early pictures it carries the name of the United States Hotel.

Page 13: On this page the book identifies John Austin's profession as that of saloon keeper. It also states that Charles Hazard moved a two-story building from Ladore to the northern side of Johnson Ave., next to Finus Smith's hotel, and operated it as a saloon. Hazard's saloon also has the distinction of hosting the first Presbyterian church service in Parsons, sheets covering the shelves of bottles of liquor on the wall.

The north side of Johnson Ave. (Main), looking west from Riggs Ave. (Central). In this picture dating from 1872 in Parsons can be seen the United States Hotel on the corner. Charles Hazard's saloon was located farther west up the block.

Page 13:   Also on page 13 the book notes that Dr. C.B. Kennedy moved a livery stable from Ladore and located it on lot 110 in Parsons. This lot later had the Catholic Church built on it.

Page 30:   Thomas C. Cory, who had moved to Parsons from Ladore in 1871, had, in 1872, his brick residence house (perhaps the first in Neosho County) torn down and rebuilt as the first brick residence in Parsons.

In addition to the buildings and the businesses, Ladore contributed several prominent early founding citizens of the new town. Each contributed something to the founding and character of Parsons and helped to build the town. What follows are some quotes and profiles of these people and their accomplishments.

M.M. Neely and Dr. A.F. Neely:

Captain Moses McKinley (M.M.) Neely and his brother Dr. A.F. Neely were early settlers in Neosho County in the 1860's before they migrated to Parsons shortly after its founding. The Osage Mission *Journal* mentions that Capt. Neely served 4 years in the 16th Kansas Cavalry. In September, 1868 he became the partner of his brother in the drug store in Osage Mission under the name of A.F. Neely & Co. Dr. Neely was the firt physician in Osage Mission [Cutler]. Shortly thereafter they brothers Neely opened a store in Ladore and Capt. Neely is mentioned several times in conjunction with that store and as postmaster of the town.

An item published in the New Chicago *Transcript* of June 10, 1871 covers the planning of a Fourth of July meeting for the Settlers' Protective Association, to be held at Parsons, rather than Ladore. Capt. Neely is listed as a member of the Committee of Arrangements for that meeting. Thus, at least one of the brothers Neely was an active member in the S.P.A. The Parsons *Sun* of March 14, 1874, in its article commemorating the third anniversary of Parsons, puts Capt. Neely's "official" arrival in Parsons as November 25, 1872.

By May of 1873 the Parsons *Herald* ran an ad/profile mentioning Capt. Neely as a dry goods / grocer in Parsons with a "large stock." The Fort Scott *Monitor* on August 14, 1873 in an article on Parsons news mentioned that Capt. Neely was in the process of remodeling the St. Charles Hotel into a "1st class grocery store." The Parsons *Surprise* of March 14, 1874 located M.M. Neely as being in business at the corner of Riggs & Johnson (now Central & Main). In the Parsons *Sun*'s 50-year anniversary issue of March 7, 1921, it was mentioned that Neely had bought the corner where the Commercial Bank was later located. These would all seem to reference the northwest corner of Central & Main, where the former United States Hotel was located. It would seem to have changed names to the St. Charles Hotel, and by 1873 had been remodeled to become M.M. Neely's store.

As to the character of Capt. Neely as a businessman, the March 1921 article in the *Sun* put forth that Mr. Neely had one of the largest stores in Ladore. He was characterized in 1869 while doing business in Ladore by the Osage Mission *Journal* as "doing a good business" and being "upright and accommodating" as well as selling goods "as cheap as anyone." The Chanute *Tribune*, in a remembrance of Ladore published on February 28, 1901, mentioned that the "boys" of Ladore would gather at Capt. Neely's store to "talk of girls" and tell and play jokes on each other.

In the political arena, in addition to his membership in the Settlers' Protective Association, M.M. Neely is mentioned by the Osage Mission *Journal* as having chaired the meeting in Ladore in November, 1869 for the purpose of calling for the end of the repeated elections for county seat in Neosho County between Erie and Osage Mission. A move at the time, if it would have succeeded, would have placed the county seat at Osage Mission (now St. Paul). In conjunction with John Hall and George W. Gabriel, he is mentioned as working for the railroad interests of the Ladore Town site in June 1870, so he was also actively working to obtain the junction of the M.K.&T. railroad divisions at Ladore.

Dr. Gabriel was both a business partner and brother-in-law to both Capt. Neely and Dr. A.F. Neely. Dr. Neely from all appearances focused more on the drug store business and on his career as a doctor. He is mentioned in the Osage Mision *Journal* in April of 1870 as treating the injuries of a drunken man in Ladore who had gotten himself beaten and had his leg broken in a fight. In March of 1874, the *Sun* mentions he and Dr. Gabriel as being sent for in conjunction with treating Anthony Amend, the father-in-law of one John Pierce. Amend had been shot and killed by Mr. Pierce in Jacksonville, Kansas, about 8 miles north and east of Parsons.

NEELY & DISCH

Wholesale and retail

DEALERS IN

DRUGS, MEDICINES,

Paints,

AND OILS,

PERFUMERIES,

Toilet Articles, Patent Medicines

BRUSHES, SOAPS, &c.

Prescriptions carefully compounded at all times.

RIGGS AVENUE,

Opposite B.A. Aldrich & Bro.

PARSONS, - - - KANSAS

M. M. NEELY

Dealer in

STAPLE AND FANCY

DRY GOODS,

Clothing,

HATS and CAPS,

Boots and Shoes,

CHOICE GROCERIES,

PROVISIONS

NOTIONS &c.

Corner of Riggs and Johnson Avenues,

PARSONS, KANSAS.

> # OSAGE LAND AGENCY,
>
> **Parsons, Labette Co., Kansas.**
>
> ———————◆———————
>
> # M. M. NEELY & CO.
>
> ### AGENTS
>
> **Office in the SUN Building**
>
> ———————◆———————
>
> **LANDS SHOWN TO PARTIES WISHING TO BUY FREE OF CHARGE.**

The advertisement images were reconstructed from advertisements in the Parsons *Sun* and Parsons *Herald* of the early 1870s.

In civic and political affairs, Dr. Neely is mentioned as being a signer of a petition to nominate T.C. Cory for mayor of Parsons in March of 1876 in the *Sun* and was called as a witness for the state in the case of State of Kansas vs. Charles H. Kimball, in January of 1878. The case was a forgery charge against Mr. Kimball in the matter of allegedly forging T.C. Cory's name (Cory was at that time Kimball's legal partner) on the charter documents for the proposed narrow gauge railroad that some were trying to have built from Parsons east to Cherokee at the time. The *Sun* noted at the time that Dr. Neely was not present at the trial to appear as a witness. Dr. Neely is also listed in the Parsons History book on page 17 as serving as mayor of Parsons from 1891 – 1895.

Thomas Cantwell (T.C.) Cory:

To get the feel and flavor of T.C. Cory's life, the opening paragraph of his obituary, printed in the Parsons *Sun* on June 21, 1888, serves to both summarize and set the table for any biography of the man.

--"Thomas C. Cory, who died at Oswego Wednesday night, was one of the brightest and most chivalric attorneys belonging to the bar of this county and news of his death was received with sadness by a large circle of friends in every part of the county. He was born in Cranberry Township, Crawford County, Ohio, July 6, 1838, where he resided until July 1861, when he enlisted in Company I, 15th Ohio and served until the 14th of February 1865."

- Parsons *Sun*, June 21, 1888, "Death of T.C. Cory"

Cory was just about to turn the age of 50 at the time of his death. However, in looking over the newspaper record in Neosho and Labette counties and in looking over the war record of the 15th Ohio Volunteers, it can be said that Mr. Cory led an eventful and most accomplished life.

The obituary in the *Sun* further notes that Cory was wounded a total of seven times during his service in the Civil War. He mustered in as a corporal in Company I at the age of 23 on September 7th, 1861. Three of his battle wounds occurred in consecutive months during May – July, 1864 at the Battle of Pickett's Mill, the Battle of Pine Knob and the Battle of Peach Tree Creek, respectively. The 15th Ohio was also involved in the Battles of Chickamauga, Shiloh, Stone's River, Chattanooga, Atlanta and many other actions and engagements in the western theater during the war. It was noted that he was discharged due to the effect of his accumulated wounds on February 14, 1865. As was noted in his obituary, he was never fully able to recover from his war wounds, the *Sun* stating that his wounds **"gradually undermined his** constitution and prevented him from ever becoming robust." However, among the many superalitives applied to him over the course of his life, the *Sun* obituary testified to his **"wonderful nerve and grit"** in building up his law practice until his health broke and he abandoned his law practice for a farmer's life.

After his war service, Cory attended the Cincinnati Law College. Upon graduation, he migrated to Kansas, settling in Canfield Township in Neosho County. In 1867 when Neosho County was divided into Neosho and Labette counties and the governments and offices for both then reorganized, Cory was appointed as the first county attorny for Neosho County; a position for which he would later win election, twice. In August, 1868, he married Miss Polly Comstock in Canfield Township and over the years had four children, Maud, Leroy, Clarissa and Paul.

Articles in the various newspapers, most particularly the Osage Mission *Journal*, have Cory shifting operations to the town of Osage Mission sometime in 1868. He served as county attorney while there, as a town trustee, and serving for a brief time as the local school teacher in the Osage Mission school until the press of business was too much for doing both jobs. However, Cory maintained a dedication to education and learning through his life. The Parsons History book notes he was appointed the clerk of Parsons School District #33 in March of 1872. In an article in the Thayer *Head Light* of March 11, 1874, commemorating the third anniversary of Parsons, Cory delivered the response to the toast "Our Schools." As stated in the *Head Light*:

--"He showed the importance of educating the moral as well as the mental and intellectual faculties. He pointed to the school house of Parsons with pride, and said when he passed from earth he asked no better monument to his memory than to have it said he did what he could to sustain the schools of Parsons."

- Thayer *Head Light*, March 11, 1874, Parsons! Third Anniversary of the Founding of the City"

As a further note to his commitment to teaching, learning and knowledge, the Parsons *Sun* of November 8, 1877 noted his name as serving on the founding Board of Directors of the Parsons Library Association.

In his personal life, Cory lived in Osage Mission until about 1870, when he moved to the town of Ladore. The "History of Neosho and Wilson Counties" by L. Wallace Duncan (as well as other sources) noted that while at Ladore he had built a two story brick residence, attributing it as perhaps the first private residence built of brick in Neosho County. Later, after moving to Parsons, he had this house taken down in Ladore and rebuilt in Parsons.

His profession made Cory a very visible man in southeast Kansas, and Cory was not one to avoid big issues either professionally or politically. As early as 1869, Cory was speaking and organizing in the settlers' cause on the question of land claims in the Osage Ceded Lands. When the railroad companies had their lawyers at the land office to challenge individual settler's claims to their land and home, T.C. Cory would often be there as well to respond to the companies on behalf of the settlers. The Osage Mission *Journal* of September 9, 1869 carried one story of such a claim dispute in which Cory was representing the settler against the railroad. Cory was among the residents in Neosho and Labette counties who organized the early settlers' meetings in Jacksonville and other towns to discuss the land question and what to do about it. It was these meetings that eventually led to the founding of the Settlers' Protective Association, and Cory himself was also a member of that association.

On numerous occasions Cory would be called upon to write or speak on behalf of the settlers of the Osage Ceded Lands. On September 15, 1870, the Osage Mission *Journal* published a letter to the editor of that paper, written by Cory, detailing the difference between the Osage Trust Lands and the Osage Ceded Lands and noting the effect of a court decision at that time on the filing of claims in the Osage Trust. In the January 19, 1871 issue of the

Parsons *Anti-Monopolist*, Cory again wrote a letter that was published, detailing the points of the legal case by which the settlers were seeking to apply the pre-emption and homestead laws to the sections in the Osage Ceded Lands and against the land grant to the railroad companies. A speech he gave at an S.P.A. meeting in Parsons on June 23, 1872 was printed in its entirety in the Thayer *Head Light* on July 13, 1872. During that speech Cory articulated the character of the people in the S.P.A. and their purpose by saying:

--"This is not a meeting of the common rabble, nor of a political faction clamorous to advance the interests of some leader, but a meeting of the intelligent masses of the people on the Osage Ceded Lands, not for the purpose of killing, burning, or destroying the lives or property of any person or corporation, but to devise means for the protection of their homes and property from the avaricious grasp of greedy Railroad Corporations and the treachery of Department officers."

- Thayer *Head Light*, July 13, 1872, "An Address"

At the celebrations after the legal victories of the settlers in the Kansas District Court in 1874 and the U.S. Supreme Court in 1876 against the railroad companies, Cory was on the list of those luminaries addressing the people in the celebrations that followed.

In Parsons Cory was partnered with various lawyers over the years, one of them being Charles Kimball. He was a member of the Parsons Pioneer Association, consisting of those citizens who had been in Parsons in 1871 or before. The Pioneer Association would organize the celebration each March 8th to commemorate the founding of the city. In the early days Cory would often chair the celebration, as well as making speeches and toasts at each occasion. He was apparently not afraid to appear in public in various roles at costumed balls and celebrations. For the 1876 Centennial Fourth of July celebration in Parsons, he was cast to play the role of General George Washington in a recreation of the end of the Battle of Yorktown which was part of the activities of the celebration that day (Parsons *Sun* June – July 1876 in advertisements for the event and in a summary article published July 15, 1876). He was among the publishers and editors of a short lived paper, the *Western Enterprise*, and in the spring of 1876 at the request of a petition filed by many citizens, he ran for mayor against the incumbent, another former Ladore resident, Dr. George Gabriel, and lost. Later, about two years before his death in 1888, he ran for the office of County Attorney of Labette County, won the election, and was serving in that office at the time of his death.

Tombstone of Thomas (T.C.) Cory, Oakwood
Cemetery, Parsons, Kansas

Civil War veterans' memorial, Oakwood Cemetery, Parsons, Kansas.

The funeral, as reported in the June 21, 1888 issue of the *Sun* was a very large and elaborate affair; the attendance for the event being estimated by the paper as "fully 3,000 people." He was buried in the G.A.R. (Grand Army of the Republic) grounds in Oakwood Cemetery in Parsons with full military honors. Despite his prominence, however, he was buried using a simple soldier's headstone, common to that area of the cemetery in Parsons.

The following resolution was adopted on the occasion of the death of T.C. Cory and published in the *Sun*.

--'"WHEREAS, we have learned with profound sorrow of the removal from our midst, by death, of Thomas Cantwell Cory, which occurred on the morning of the 14th inst.;

Therefore be it resolved by the people of the city of Parsons, in public meeting assembled, that in the death of our fellow townsman, Thomas C. Cory, the community has lost a good citizen, the country a loyal defender, the legal profession a member who was a credit to the bar, the county of Labette a zealous and capable public officer, each one of us a good friend, his sadly bereaved family a loving and devoted husband and father and that we extend to his family our profound sympathy and condolence in this, their sad and terrible affliction and while deeply mourning the death of our friend we humbly bow to the will of an all wise Providence.

That a copy of this resolution be furnished to the family of the deceased and also copies to the press of Labette and Neosho counties with the request that the same be published.'

Committee: S.L. Coulter, C.M. Kimball, C.B. Kennedy, H.M. Carr, and V.J. Knapp.'

- Parsons *Sun*, June 21, 1888, "The T.C. Cory Obsequies"

Dr. C.B. Kennedy:

Dr. Clempson B. Kennedy was not as actively involved in the public life of Parsons as some of the other "Ladorians" being described in this narrative. However, he was a well known doctor, owner of a livery stable for some time and a businessman in Parsons. He also had invested and involved himself in real estate on the town site, there being three additions on the northern part of town that, at least in part, bear his name. For a time, most of the northern part of Parsons, bounded on the south by what became Gabriel Avenue, was owned by Dr. Kennedy. The region partly consisting of Kennedy's First and Second Additions was described and referred to as "Kennedy's Grove" in an 1874 article in the Parsons *Sun* as the site of the biggest of the settlers' mass meetings that took place as the Settlers' Protective Association pursued its legal battle against the M.K.&T. and L.L.&G. railroads. Attendance at the meeting in 1874 was estimated at over 10,000 people at a time when most towns in the Osage Ceded Lands would have numbered around a 1,000 people or less.

The newspaper articles and the Parsons History book fix the time of Dr. Kennedy's opening of his livery stable on Riggs Avenue (Central) as November, 1870. It is further stated in the record that St. Patrick's Catholic Church was later built on that location. Dr. Gabriel recalled in a remembrance published in the *Sun* in 1920 his buying lots from Dr. Kennedy upon which he had his first home in Parsons, before buying the house at the northeast corner of Riggs and Crawford.

The northern part of Parsons from the 1887 Atlas, showing Kennedy's First and Second Additions and the Felix & Kennedy Addition, as well as land owned by Dr. Kennedy on either side of Labette Creek.

The streets running through Felix & Kennedy's Addition are Gabriel, Kennedy, Felix and Fellows avenues.

The obituary in the Parsons *Sun* on August 17, 1908 lists Dr. Kennedy's residence as 418 N. Central, and the 50th Anniversary edition of the Parsons *Sun* of March 7, 1921 notes that his wife still was living at that location. The Parsons *Herald* of May 29, 1873 notes that Dr. Gabriel and Dr. Kennedy shared an office on Riggs Avenue at that time. In July of 1875 there was a major fire in downtown Parsons that destroyed several buildings, including Dr. Kennedy's.

Dr. Kennedy was born on May 24, 1837 in the town of Hanford, in Ohio. He attended Rush Medical College in Philadelphia and practiced as a doctor for a time before serving in the Civil War as a surgeon in the army. He migrated to Kansas in 1868, living in Topeka until 1870 before moving to Erie and then to Ladore. He married Mattie Cambern, the daughter of the first Presbyterian preacher in Parsons, H.H. Cambern, on March 8, 1871, the same day the first lots in Parsons were sold. He and his wife moved to Parsons from Ladore after their marriage.

The obituary further notes that he practiced as a physician in Parsons for twenty years.

The Parsons *Sun* stated the following as to his life in Parsons and his character:

--"Here he practiced his profession for twenty years, successfully and honorably, and his entire life has been one of honor and integrity in every business, personal or professional transaction. Here his children were born, and his faith in Parsons brought rich rewards in the large holding of Parsons property which he had at the time of his death, being one of the largest property owners in the city.

- Parsons *Sun*, August 17, 1908, "Death of a Pioneer"

Dr. George Gabriel:

Of all the people who moved from Ladore to Parsons, perhaps none had greater impact, nor had lived a more fulfilled life, than Dr. George W. Gabriel. The bare facts of his life are these. He was born at Athens, Ohio, on November 17, 1841. He enlisted to fight in the Civil War in 1862, serving in Company I, 52d Reg., Ohio Vol. Inf., and later in the 75th and 116th Ohio regiments and was at the battles of Gettysburg and Antietam, among others. He came to Kansas in 1864 and enlisted in the 17th Kansas Infantry, Company D, and was involved in the campaign against General Price's invasion of Missouri and Kansas, fighting at the battle of Westport. He lived for a time in Topeka after the war before attending the Starling Medical College at Columbus, Ohio, returning to Kansas in 1868 and locating in Neosho County, living primarily in Ladore and practicing at that place and Osage Mission. In 1871 he graduated with an M.D. from the Kansas Medical College and then located at the new town of Parsons. He resided in Parsons for the remainder of his life, being elected six times to serve as mayor of the town, three times to serve in the state legislature and almost winning election to serve as U.S. Senator. He was active in many community and civic organizations and was particularly active in politics with the Democratic Party, serving, in addition to his elective offices previously listed, as chairman of various party committees on numerous occasions. He died on April 29, 1930 at the age of 88. Dr. Gabriel was twice married, first to Elizabeth Hager at Ladore in 1869 and second to Mary Brown in 1897, and had two surviving children, Harry and Mary.

Just in summary, Dr. Gabriel led a full life, but it becomes even more interesting when examined in more detail. The Parsons *Sun* in March 1920 profiled Dr. Gabriel in its March 12th issue and upon the paper's request Dr. Gabriel wrote a memoir of his 50 years in Parsons and his time in Kansas, which was printed in the paper's March 19th issue. The record shows that Dr. Gabriel served as mayor in Parsons from 1875-77, 1881-83, 1883-85, 1887-89, 1903-05, and 1905-07. During his terms as mayor the first brick and stone sidewalks were laid, the water works franchise was established, the first gas franchise, the first light franchise and the first sewer system in Parsons was put in. In addition to being elected to mayor and the city council on numerous occasions, he was elected and served three terms in the Kansas House and one term in the Kansas Senate. It can be truly said that Dr. Gabriel had an influence the growth and development of the town of Parsons for over thirty years in political life.

Prior to his time in Parsons, Mr. Gabriel recounted many incidents during his time in the 17th Kansas, the people he met and the incidents he witnessed. He wrote of the difficult life of both soldier and settler in Kansas at that time, of long nights traveling while on duty while suffering from lack of food and poor conditions. He wrote of coming upon a group of soldiers in one company who had lynched a member of their company over a disagreement over a gambling debt. He mentioned several times the lawless conditions that made travel at that time difficult from town to town in eastern Kansas. At one point, when assigned to take 11 prisoners from the fort his unit had constructed on the grounds in Lawrence where the University of Kansas now stands (Mt. Oread) to Paola and bring back supplies, he first asked for escort due to the country being "full of bushwhackers", and since escort wasn't available, requested he be allowed to select his own group of drivers. Dr. Gabriel recounted the affair as follows:

--"I selected as my drivers three men, one of them being Jacob Flint, a full-blooded Shawnee Indian; another Stephen Blue Jacket, a full-blood Delaware Indian; and the third, "Batt" Moriarty, the father of C.H. Moriarty of this city. I then handcuffed all my prisoners together by their hands and feet, placed them in the middle wagon partly with hay and chained them fast to the wagon; and as that was before the days of prohibition, I got a quart of whiskey, gave each of the drivers a drink and we started. Some of the prisoners wanted a drink; but as they were mean enough without it, I cut their part of it out. Each wagon was driven by six mules. Flint was in the lead, Moriarty was in the middle with the prisoners and Blue Jacket in the rear. Each man was armed with two revolvers and a carbine and the quart of whiskey."

- Parsons *Sun*, March 19, 1920, "Fifty Years Ago"

During his memoir, he remembered the engagements his unit had with the Confederate troops under General Price, during their raid into Kansas in 1864. His unit, as he recalled, was engaged at Westport, then at battles at Pleasanton and Mine Creek and finally at Dry Wood, Missouri.

Between mustering out in November of 1864 and returning for a time to Ohio to study medicine, Dr. Gabriel spent time as a wagon driver along the old Santa Fe Trail, driving wagons between Topeka and Fort Union, New Mexico. He told a story of encountering bands of hostile Cheyenne Indians, led by Old Black Kettle, and losing cattle and oxen from the wagon train as the Indians attempted several times to stampede their cattle. After this incident, he was hired to ride through southern Kansas to collect election returns that had not been returned to Topeka in December 1865. He rode through Woodson, Greenwood, Allen and Neosho counties on this trip, seeing the country for the first time where he would later make his home.

Upon returning to Kansas, he arrived in Osage Mission in March, 1868 and on the first of May located at Fort Roach / Ladore, taking quarters at James N. Roach's house "Fort Roach." For the next two years he was the "country doctor" riding on call from farm to farm and from town to town as the need arose for his services. His recollections of some of his encounters during that time give portrait to the difficulty of life for the early settlers in southeast Kansas. His obituary in the *Sun* mentioned that Gabriel would **"have his breakfast at Ladore, his noon meal at what became Parsons and his evening meal in Osage Mission."** In addition to treating the people in southern Neosho County and Labette County, the obituary also mentioned that Gabriel would travel down into the Indian Territory to treat sick Indians.

He was at Ladore during the Ladore Tragedy in 1870. Newspaper accounts and his own recollection show that it was to his home that James N. Roach came to give news of what the gang was doing. He was part of the party that first located some of the gang and was there when the lynchings took place. He remembers that before the lynching **"You could look up the street at almost any time of the day or night and see from one to half a dozen fights going on. I had ridden down the streets more than once and seen fellows being robbed in the full light of day,"** and how the town became more orderly and the criminal activity in the area largely disappeared after the events of that night in May, 1870.

Dr. Gabriel seemed to see his share of lynching in Kansas. In the army he saw the lynching of one soldier by others in his company over a gambling dispute, he was in Ladore when that terrible affair took place, and in March of 1874 he and Dr. Neely were called to the town of Jacksonville, about 8 miles north and east of Parsons, to attempt to treat a man named Amend, who had been shot by his son-in-law, John Pierce. Amend had confronted Pierce over how Pierce was treating his children, and Pierce shot Amend in McCaslin's store in Jacksonville. By the time Dr. Gabriel arrived in Jacksonville, Amend had died and a group of vigilantes had taken Pierce from where he was being held for trial in the Jacksonville schoolhouse and hanged him from a tree near Hickory Creek, west of the town.

In his memoir, Dr. Gabriel remembers the events of the night of the Pierce lynching:

--"I went into the house to warm before I started back and in a few moments they brought the fellow in. The court was getting ready to perform its functions when I happened to notice a fellow who lived west of this place stretch himself up and look in at the door. In an instant every light in the house went out and when they relighted them the prisoner was gone. I at once made up my mind that I was warm enough and the best thing I could do was to get home. Down the road about a mile I found the fellow hanging to a limb of a tree, dead. I did not stop to take time to make any inquiry but took the straightest road home."

- Parsons *Sun*, March 19, 1920, "Fifty Years Ago"

In addition to his political service and medical service as a citizen in Parsons, the *Sun* in its 1930 obituary notes his involvement in various other organizations and clubs.

--"Masonry in Parsons owes its existence, in part, to Dr. Gabriel, who was a charter member of Parsons lodge No. 117; the Parsons chapter, No. 39, Royal Arch Masons and Knights Templar No. 17, Coeur de Lion Commandery. He was past commander of the commandery and for seven years was master of the Blue lodge from its first year. He was also a charter member of the local Eastern Star lodge and a member of the Knights of Pythias and Odd Fellows."

- Parsons *Sun*, April 30, 1930, "First Physician of Parsons, Dr. Gabriel is Dead"

The esteem with which he was held in Parsons is expressed several times in the *Sun* obituary and in other articles of the period. The *Sun* stated:

--"Thousands of persons in Parsons and other towns in this vicinity have received medical care at the hands of the pioneer doctor and in each patient he made a friend."

--"In the death of the pioneer physician and city builder Parsons loses one of its foremost citizens, a man who has been an outstanding civic leader and public figure in this state, and a man whose history from early life is the history of this city because he was here before Parsons was founded."
--"Never, perhaps, has there been a Parsons man who was more highly respected or more universally well liked."

--"Enduring the hardships of the early days with the other hardy settlers of this city, he toiled with them side by side and deserves the tribute that he was one of the finest and most valuable men the city ever had."

- Parsons *Sun*, April 30, 1930, "First Physician of Parsons, Dr. Gabriel is Dead"

As an honor and tribute to Dr. Gabriel, when the city was planning its 55th anniversary celebration in 1926, it was decided to appoint a "King" of Parsons for the week of planned activities, and an accompanying "Queen." The choice was obvious, and Dr. Gabriel was appointed "King of Parsons" with his grand-daughter, Elizabeth Noyes, serving as Queen.

He's King of All That He Surveys This Week

Dr. George W. Gabriel.

From the Parsons *Daily Republican*, March 7, 1926, on the 55th Anniversary of Parsons, Kansas

**Tombstone of Dr. George W. Gabriel and family in
Oakwood Cemetery, Parsons, Kansas.**

Part of the remembrance of Ladore must be in the people that lived there and what they were able to accomplish. Men like the Neely brothers, T.C. Cory, and Dr. Gabriel did much to make of Parsons the success it was in its early days. Had the M.K.&T. elected to establish itself at Ladore, who can doubt but similar achievement by these men would have been associated with that place? This summary of some of the more notable Ladorians / Parsonians will close with the conclusion stated by Dr. Gabriel in his 1920 memoir in the Parsons *Sun*.

--"After having seen Kansas grow as I have and all that has been in life for me, either success or failure, joy or sorrow, have come to me here, and a great portion of it in the city of Parsons. Is it to be wondered at that I at least think that there is no state like Kansas and no city like Parsons?"

- Parsons *Sun*, March 19, 1920, "Fifty Years Ago"

Who knows but for a different decision by the M.K.&T. that Dr. Gabriel would have said the same thing about Ladore?

Chapter 8: Remembering Ladore

Judge Roach after the Fall of Ladore

In remembering Ladore it is of interest to focus in on the founder of the place, James N. Roach, once again. In reviewing the articles for details of his life in Neosho County after the events of 1870 and the moving of the buildings of Ladore to Parsons, it must be noted that Mr. Roach's life did not get any the less colorful in the succeeding years before his removal from Kansas to the Indian Territory.

In 1871, as reported in the Neosho County (formerly Osage Mission) *Journal*, the Judge's name as reported indirectly in connection with the disappearance of two men in the area of Ladore. Both were reported in the *Journal* on September 9, 1871 under the headline "FOUL PLAY!" The first, a German farm worker named John Martin, was reported missing in June of 1871. Roach stated in the article that he owed Martin for two month's work at the time of the disappearance and that all belongings except his clothing had been left behind. The second, one John Arbuckle, was reported last seen on the railroad track near Roach's house. From the articles known at this point, no trace of the men was found.

As was mentioned at the conclusion of the chapter on the Ladore Tragedy, Judge Roach was up for trial on charges of assault in the winter term of the district court in 1871. The result of these legal proceedings has already been noted, Judge Roach being acquitted of one charge and the other being dismissed. However, a brief notice in the Neosho County *Journal* on December 9th is worth noting, inasmuch as it gives some indication as to Roach's social status in the area, at least so far as the local press was concerned.

--"Judge J.N. Roach, usually known in these parts by the endearing name "Old Fort," has been in the city during the week attending to legal business. We are sorry to learn that the Judge intends to throw up his extensive legal practice and in the future give his whole attention to his quiet home and the farm on the tragic banks of the Labette."

- Neosho County *Journal*, December 9, 1871

To date, no record of Judge Roach having obtained that title officially in Kansas (even though it has been found that he was a justice of the peace in Indiana), so one must assume that the editor of the *Journal* was making a joking reference to the two assault cases for which Roach was in Osage Mission to stand trial.

Mr. Roach shows up again in the papers in January, 1872, in a local news item on the 27th of that month for which he was interviewed while in Osage Mission for a few days. The editor of the Neosho County *Journal* refers to Roach as a "staunch Republican." The news item related the news that the tendency of Democratic newspaper editors to not pay for their lodging at his boarding house, and to not even do the courtesy of leaving a copy of their paper, was causing him to decide he would not change his political leanings from Republican to Democrat. The quote that concludes the article was **"he is of the opinion that such base ingratitude could exist only in hearts of democratic proclivity."**

An item on Ladore's demise was published in the Thayer *Head Light* on July 27, 1872 that mentions Mr. Roach indirectly. As the news item is both noteworthy as to the state of the former town two years after the establishment of Parsons and is fairly short, it is quoted in its entirety here.

--"LADORE—This classic place is fast falling back to its old point in population, and its pristine splendor is returning. We saw another house on wheels, moving in the direction of Parsons, following the track of all those who have gone that way before it. We suggest that Smith & Son, and old man Roach, hold a convention of themselves, and change the name back to *Ft. Roach*. This is certainly more appropriate."

- Thayer Head Light, July 27, 1872, "Ladore"

This article effectively states that the town site had apparently largely returned to its state of the year 1868 in that there were but few, if any, houses or buildings left on the town site, other than James Roach's house and few others.

A correspondent for the Lawrence *Western Home Journal* of October 17th, 1872, on a journey through southeastern Kansas to write profiles of the various cities, encountered "Old Fort" Roach on the train trip to Osage Mission. The correspondent refers to Roach as an "old comrade" and mentions that Roach was intending to run as an independent Republican candidate for the Kansas House from the 45th district. The author closes the article with his wishes for Roach's success. Roach's quest for the nomination at the 45th District convention was also covered in the Osage Mission *Transcript* of October 11 and 25, 1872, referring to Roach as "one of the old, original free soilers". Despite his hopes of vigorous support by the Ladore delegation, Roach lost the nomination to Elijah Cravens on a vote of 11 to 5.

The year 1873 turned out to be an active year for Mr. Roach so far as the newspapers in southeast Kansas were concerned, and not for terribly positive reasons. Just after the April elections that year, Judge Roach took paper to pen to crow over the defeat of his fellow Ladore and Fort Roach resident, and author of the Fort Roach Eye-Teams columns of several years before, Lewis Reese in the recent elections. The office for which Reese was running is not entirely clear from the letters, but Roach is entirely happy about it, just the same. As there are few samples known of Mr. Roach's writing, the exchange of letters and the disagreement with the editors of the Neosho County *Journal*, as they were published in the Thayer *Head Light* on April 16, 23, and 30, 1873 are included in their entirety. The spelling and diction are left as they were printed.

--"Ladore, Kas.   APRIL 1st, '73

EDITOR HEAD-LIGHT: Glory enough for one day, the champion of Liberalism defeated, ex-typo Mountdianthis Saber Rease defeated for justice by an overwhelming majority. No Republicans in the field, but we plaid _____ with his ducks, we took up a Confederate candidate from Sumner County and beat him bad. He needed a funeral procession, but failed to have sufficient friends to form a corporal's guard, and so he has to lay on the *terra firma* and stink. He has lost his foul hold and God only can tell what he will do next, for he can't expect an appointment from the President or Governor, and so you and I and all good Republicans will have to say farewell to Mount dianthis Saber ex-typo Rease — ex-justice of Ladore T.T. Rease.

Yours,   J.N.R."

- Thayer *Head Light*, April 16, 1873

--"The Thayer *Head-Light*, of the 19th, contains a communication from Ladore, signed "J.N.R." in which the writer tries to ridicule Louis A. Reese, Esq., of that township. Mr. Reese is one of the oldest and best citizens of Neosho County, and is held in the highest esteem by his neighbors, and the writer of the article in question it a personal enemy of Mr. Reese."

- Thayer *Head Light*, April 23, 1873, "Osage Mission"

--"Ladore, Kas.   April 24, 1873

EDITOR HEAD-LIGHT: I see after a careful perusal of the *Journal* of the 16th that a celebrated and much respected sheet, and my old and familiar paper has seen fit to defend L.A. Reese. I am glad he has some defence, but I wish the *Journal* would tell the truth when he said that

Mr. Rease was one of the oldest and best settlers in the country, and held by his neighbors as such. The *Journal* knew that was false; and when he said the writer of the article in the *Head Light* of the 16th was a personal enemy of Mr. Reese, he was saying something he knew nothing about. Personally I care very little about Mr. Rease, politically and religiously—I hate him, or any other such man; and so far as his neighborship is concerned, he is very much like myself, his financial proclivities is too limited to accommodate any person; this is no sin for him or me either, but I do think and say—that the people of the township acted wise, when they tilted him overboard at the last election. As the *Journal* thinks he is the oldest and most respected citizen of this county, I will just refer him to the poll books and then to the District Clerk's docket, and see if he can find one case of an appeal from the said justice, but what has been reversed on exceptions, and the cause was either prejudice or pure ignorance, and my opinion is, it was both mixed up, and if my opinion is correct the world can judge how decisions came and how they was upset before an impartial judge. Mr. *Journal* you had better come over before you spend too much breath, you can have a free dinner and a social chat, and I would be glad to see you, but stick to the truth and your petitions will be heard, and you rewarded for your labors.

J.N.R."

Thayer *Head Light*, April 30, 1873

Whatever may or may not have come from this exchange barbs over the result of the 1873 spring elections, Judge Roach's affairs in 1873 became decidedly more complicated socially and legally through the spring of 1873 as the affair of "The Bloody Benders" broke over southeast Kansas just two weeks later.

The Bloody Benders and the Roach Family

In late 19th century southeas Kansas there are three major "crime" stories in the folklore of the region. One is the Ladore Tragedy of 1870, the massacre of the Dalton gang in Coffeyville in the 1890's, and perhaps most infamous of all, the Bloody Benders of 1873. Of the Bender affair it should be noted that even up to the present day (2013) there are still books being written and movies being planned or filmed over the family of serial killers who resided in western Labette County during the early 1870's. The highlights of the affair will be covered here, as the aftermath of the affair does affect the Roach family of Ladore, however an exhaustive coverage of the case and all of the legend, speculation and rumor that have been created about it since, will be left for the time being to the books and stories already in existence.

The first victim that historically has been attributed to the Benders, based on how the murder was performed with slit throat and head smashed in, was reported in the Thayer *Head Light* on October 26, 1872 and the Osage Mission *Transcript* of November 1, 1872. A man by the name of Jones was found dead in "Big Hill Creek, on the farm of R.M. Bennett, Liberty Township." The man's throat had been cut and his head crushed with a blow to the right side of the head. Over the next few months many people were reported as disappearing and not to be heard from again in Labette County. All were known to be traveling the main road from Independence, Kansas in Montgomery County to Osage Mission in Neosho County. The Bender family had a small cabin / store / hotel along the trail, about 10 miles or so west of Parsons. The claim lies just north of the current U.S. 400 highway and is centrally located between the towns of Parsons, Cherryvale and Thayer. Certain travelers were targeted as they stopped at the Benders' hotel while traveling, they were murdered there and buried in the orchard near the Bender home.

The affair broke in the second week of May, 1873 due to the massive hunt undertaken for Dr. William York of Indepence, brother of prominent state senator A.M. York, also of

Independence, who had gone missing while hunting others who had gone missing along the trail to Osage Mission. In all, there were 8 to 9 victims found in shallow graves on the Bender claim, with more suspected but never found. The Bender family managed to disappear into the pages of history, leaving various rumors as to their fate behind. Without the Benders to stand trial (or to be lynched), the focus shifted toward possible accomplices who might have lived in the locality. This was due to the fact that, in addition to the people, the horses, wagons, belongings that were known to be with the victims were never found, supposedly disposed of by local accomplices. Among the settlers in the area arrested on suspicion were members of the Roach family of Ladore.

The first mention of the Roach family was published in the Fort Scott *Monitor* on April 26, 1873, nearly three weeks before the Bender affair broke publicly.

--"We have been informed through a private source that the Roach family, living in Labette County [Neosho County – Ladore], at one time residents of Fort Scott, have lately been arrested on suspicion of being implicated in the recent murders in their neighborhood, the body of a man and child having been discovered in a stream near their residence."

- Fort Scott *Monitor*, April 26, 1873, "The Roach Family Arrested"

However, the Osage Mission *Transcript* of May 2, 1873 reported the story to be false and printed a letter of retraction from George Crawford, the publisher and editor of the *Monitor*.

--"Last Saturday morning there appeared in the Fort Scott *Monitor* an article stating that the "Roach family had all been arrested." We know this to be false, at the time having seen and conversed with "old Fort" and other members of the family, after the notice appeared. For personal satisfaction and public vindication, Capt. Ayers wrote to Geo. A. Crawford for particulars, receiving the following reply:

CAPT. AYERS—Dear Sir: Yours received. Say to Judge Roach that I was very sorry when I saw the unfortunate item in the paper, and had it corrected in the very next issue. The editor did not know the Judge or his family, and he only gave the story as a report or rumor. He thought his informant was reliable, but is now satisfied to the contrary.

I am very sorry and was very much displeased when the article came out. This the Judge must well know, for I have always had the most friendly feelings for him and his family and would not see them misrepresented.

Yours,

Geo. A. Crawford."

- Osage Mission *Transcript*, May 2, 1873, "The Arrest of Judge Roach"

During the reporting of the Bloody Benders that occurred in various articles through May of 1873, it was reported either that the entire Roach family had been arrested, or that Roach's son Addison had been arrested, or Addison and various other members who were sons-in-law of Roach at one time or another. Among the list included in Roach's extended family as reported in the Lawrence *Republican Journal*, the Wichita *Eagle* and other papers were John Harness, Roach's stepson from his wife's previous marriage, William Buxton, who was married to Roach's daughter Jemima, Peter Harkness, who was married to Roach's daughter Sophia, and Major John David Mefford, formerly a son-in-law to Roach through a previous marriage to Jemima Roach, and a colorful figure himself in the history of Fort Scott, Kansas and Joplin, Missouri. These Roach family members were by no means the only people arrested as many families living near the Bender claim were either questioned or arrested in suspicion of being connected in some way with the Benders.

In the aftermath of all of the arrests, no one was convicted and all were released. The tactics undertaken by the authorities were criticized in an article in the Parsons *Herald* of May 22, 1873, which summarized the results of the wide ranging arrests of citizens in Labette and Neosho counties after the Benders disappeared. Several points made in the article are shown below.

--"The one who was ten days in jail, John Harness, was brought here last Tuesday, the day for examination; but no witnesses appearing against him, and the County Attorney not even appearing to prosecute, was released."

--"As it stands the parties have been released, but their names have been published far and wide, and a stigma has naturally attached to them [that is] hard to obliterate."

--"J.N. Roach, of Ladore, has brought suit against the *Monitor*, of Fort Scott, for publishing that his family had been arrested, when such was not the case."

- Parsons *Herald*, May 22, 1873, "An Outrage"

The editor of the *Herald* also criticized the "promiscuous arresting of persons" by "irresponsible or mythical parties," and requested that the various papers who had published the names of the people arrested would also publish the fact that the persons named had been released due to lack of evidence and witnesses against them.

Later, a letter to the editor of the Parsons *Herald*, published on July 3, 1873 with author not named, took great pains to criticize Senator York and the activities of his posse subsequent to the Bender disappearance. The author of the letter made several accusations against York in the aftermath of the Bender affair. Among them were: paying or promising to pay people to swear out warrants on innocent parties; tearing down fences and tearing open farms and other acts of vandalism and petty theft; and that some of the first to aid York in the search for his brother were among the first arrested.

The author then goes on to state the report of the arrest of the Roach family is "a lie," and further accuses the people from Independence of attempting to throw suspicion of guilt onto the people of Ladore and of Osage Township in Labette County, where the Bender claim was located. The author goes into great detail in defending the members of the Roach family, though misspelling their names in many cases, as well as taking to task the arrest of many of the other families named in the previously reported articles at the time.

What can be made of the various reports mentioning and appearing to contradict the arrest of the Roach family? It appears that the early reports of arrest were erroneous, and according to the *Herald*, going to be litigated. The author of the letter to the *Herald*, while first labeling the reported arrest of the Roach family as a lie, then goes on to mention Harness and Buxton and others and their treatment after being arrested. Apparently the author did not realize the connection by marriage of these men to the Roach family. In any event, it does appear that at least some of Roach's family were arrested, but no charges and no convictions ever took place.

The only mention relative to J.N. Roach in 1874 that has so far been found is the following notice about coal exploration taking place on his farm:

--"The company organized for the purpose of searching for coal on the farm of J.N. Roach has not yet obtained the much coveted black diamonds, but are still going down for them with sanguine hopes of soon striking a deep and heavy vein."

- Fort Scott *Monitor*, May 5, 1874

As far as Ladore is concerned, there was still a community there, if not an organized town. The families around the township were still using the school and church into the 20th century, as late as the 1920's. In an article published in the Parsons *Eclipse* on September 3, 1874, Judge Roach's old rival, Louis Reese and others in the township met at Ladore to organize the Ladore Independent Club as a local branch of the Independent Reform Party movement. They passed a series of resolutions as to the dangers and corruption of the organized political parties, supported Sidney Clarke, former representative from Kansas if he would run for Congress again, and other organizational matters for the club.

In addition to this level of political activity deemed worthy of news reporting, the local chapter of the Settlers' Protective Association, Ladore Council No. 11, was still active. In what was known as the Garlinghouse Affair, which was a case of a claim dispute between N.F. Garlinghouse and wife as the supposed "jumpers" and one J.A. Gatton as the owner of record, having purchased the claim from one John Wesner according to the S.P.A. As reported in the Neosho County *Journal* on December 9, 1874, a group of S.P.A. members from both Labette and Neosho counties tried to force Garlinghouse off the claim, which was located near Jacksonville and towards the south end of what is known as the "Island" where the Neosho River splits into two channels for several miles and then rejoins near a point called Trotter's Ford. Garlinghouse and wife, as reported in the *Journal* defended themselves with shotguns and at the end of the encounter were still in possession of the claim. In articles published on December 17th in the *Eclipse* and in the *Sun* on December 26th, the Ladore Chapter No. 11 of the S.P.A. published a resolution of censure against the Neosho County *Journal*, naming the article as false, naming Garlinghouse as a claim jumper, and disputing that the group that went to confront Garlinghouse were not "ruffians" but "law-abiding citizens, in charge of their known duty."

The affair kept escalating through December, 1874 as reported in the Neosho County *Journal* in an article entitled "Mob Law"on December 24th; in the Parsons *Surprise* on December 12th, referring to the encounter and aftermath as the "Battle of the Neosho"; and in the Parsons *Eclipse* in its own article entitled "Mob Law" and also published on the 24th. As the *Journal* reported the story in a letter from one Thomas Wells, a man named Andrew Olsen was arrested in conjunction with the attack on the Garlinghouse cabin on the 6th of December and tried and fined $50 and costs on December 7th. As Wells reported in the letter to the *Journal*, the town of Jacksonville, where the trial took place and where Mr. Olsen was in custody, was surrounded by "100 men on horseback." They demanded of the local Justice of the Peace, Esquire Patterson, that the fine should be reversed and no further warrants be issued. It should be noted this was but a few months after the Pierce hanging by local vigilantes in the Jacksonville area, as well. Patterson reportedly gave in to the mob's demands. The Parsons *Surprise* story essentially agreed with the main points of the letter and noted the **"persuasive eloquence in a double barrel shotgun"** in reversing the fine and charges against Olsen.

The conclusion to the affair was reported in the Neosho County *Journal* on January 13, 1875, in an article entitled "The Garlinghouse Affair" and demonstrated the full power and functioning of the S.P.A. in adjudicating claim disputes on the Osage Ceded Lands. The Grand Council of the S.P.A. appointed a committee to investigate the competing claims for the land in question, the SE quarter of Section 7, Town 30, Range 21 in Lincoln Township. Both Gatton and Garlinghouse, as reported, signed a $1,200 bond to abide by the decision of the committee. The committee reviewed the title history of the claim and published its conclusions in favor of Gatton in the article in the *Journal* of January 13th. It also concluded that some items owned and brought onto the claim by Garlinghouse would be removable by him.

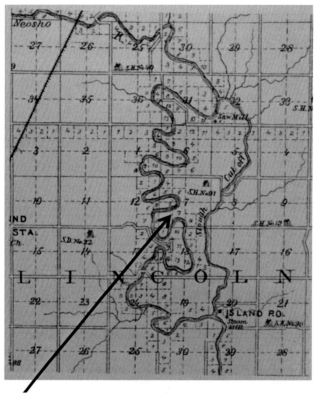

The Neosho River Island in Neosho County, Kansas, in which the river splits into two channels just southeast of Osage Mission (now St. Paul).

The SE corner of Section 7 is located near an oxbow of the western channel of the river as indicated on this section of the 1887 Kansas

J.N. Roach returns to the newspaper record with a brief mention in the Parsons *Eclipse* on February 18, 1875. The quote attributed to Roach in the brief item seems to be a response of sorts to the formation and activities of the Ladore Independent Club the previous year by his neighbor, Louis Reese.

--"J.N. Roach gave us a call this week. Fort says he still belongs to the Republican Party and is not ashamed to own it."

- Parsons Eclipse, February 18, 1875

It should be noted that the Parsons *Eclipse* began publication in 1874 and was founded by Dr. J.B. Lamb. Dr. Lamb had moved down to Parsons from Osage Mission and had opened a store in Ladore. For a time the store was operated out of J.N. Roach's boarding house.

There were various items relating to Ladore and J.N. Roach published in the area newspapers in 1875. An item in May of 1875 in the Parsons *Surprise* detailed the fight of James Shafer of Ladore to protect his crops from grasshoppers using a mixture of salt and coal oil. A lengthy letter written to the editor of the Parsons *Eclipse* of July 15th detailed the Fourth of July celebration in that vicinity that summer.

Of particular interest in tracing the actual state of affairs of the condition of the Ladore town site itself was a notice that was published in the Chanute *Times* of August 7th, titled "Notice of Sale of Land for the Delinquent Taxes of the Year 1874." The tables covered the entirety of Neosho County in terms of delinquent land for sale. Of interest here is the part covering "Ladore City." The results of the table are summarized as follows: **Owner: M. K. & T. Railway Co.; Blocks 1 – 62, Lots 1 – 12 in each block. Blocks 63 – 70, Lots 1 – 14 (in) in each block.** This effectively was the entire town site of Ladore and all of its lots. Ladore as an organized, incorporated town could be officially pronounced dead from this moment on. A local and active community of residents in the area still existed, but Ladore would exist as a school, a church, a cemetery, a small depot and post office only. A correspondent for the Thayer *Head Light* in an article published on September 17th while traveling through the area gave this description of the town site at that time:

--"LADORE – Here a broken brick and there an old boot top with post office between was all that was left to mark the site of what would have been a big town if Parsons had never been heard of. After a good deal of trouble we succeeded in getting through grass 10 feet high clear away from Laid o'er."

- Thayer *Head Light*, September 17, 1875, "Parsons"

An article in December 29, 1875 in the Fort Scott *Monitor* and another in the Osage Mission *Journal* on January 14th of 1876 regarding J.N. Roach showed him to be as colorful and as energetic as ever in his opinions and actions. The *Monitor* article in December, it was reported that Roach had sued the M.K.&T. for not giving alarm as the train crossed the public road/highway near his residence. The desired recompense was for $20 per instance for a total of 309 instances where the train had failed to give alarm while crossing the road.

In early 1876, Roach, was apparently incensed at what he felt was incompetence and corruption in the affairs of the Neosho County Bar Association and the election of one Peter Bell to be judge of the Seventh District in a controversial election for the remainder of an unexpired term. A poem was submitted to the *Journal* as a parody of the poem "The Bells" by Edgar Allen Poe.

PETER BELL

Respectfully Dedicated to the Bar of Neosho County

BY FORT ROACH

Hear Dame Justice with her BELL,
Peter Bell!
What a world of trouble now his coming does foretell!

How he rages, rages, rages,
In the courtroom day and night,
Till the bones of legal sages
That have quiet lain for ages
Fairly rattle with affright!

Keeping time, time, time,
In a grim and ghastly rhyme,
To the tintinnabulations that so terribly do well
From the Bell, Bell, Bell, Bell,
Bell, Bell, Bell,
From the snapping and the flapping of the Bell.

Hear the profound Peter Bell,
Massive Bell!
How the gobs of legal lore cause his learned head to swell!
Through the trial of a case
How he lengthens out his face!
When he enters up his notes
With solemn air,
Then what jingling wisdom floats
Round the corners and the alleys,
Like the frantic squeal of shoats
On a "tare."

Oh, from out this prince of Bells,
What a gush of greasy gas voluminously swells!
How it swells!
How it smells
Like the devil! How it tells
On a fellow till he yells
At the swinging and the ringing
Of this king of all the Bells,
Of the Bells, Bells, Bells, Bells,
Bells, Bells, Bells,
Of this might, righty-tighty-est of the Bells.

Hear the stern judicial Bell,
Peter Bell!
What a tale of wisdom now he solemnly doth tell!
How the ear of luckless wight
He doth palsy with affright,
Who, too horrified to speak
Can only shriek, shriek, shriek,
In mortal fear,
In a clamorous appealing to the mercy of the Bell,
In a mad expostulation with the deaf and solemn Bell,
Growing more and more sonorous
With his sweaty nose so porous,
And his resolute endeavor
Soon, soon to sit or never
As one of the tripedal pier.

Oh, the Bell, Bell, Bell!
What a tale his cheek doth tell
Of a galoot!
How he clangs and rings and roars!
How the gushing sweat outpours
From the tip-end of his palpitating snoot!
Yet the eye it fully knows,
By his sweating
And his fretting
How his Honor ebbs and flows;
Yet the eye distinctly knows
In the jangling
And the wrangling
How the stern decision goes
By the flushing and the gushing of his Honor's classic nose,
Oh, the Bell,
Oh, the Bell, Bell, Bell, Bell,
Bell, Bell, Bell,
Oh, if Atchison had *only* beat thee, Bell!

Hear the judgments of the Bell,
Sapient Bell!
What beautiful reversals their conclusions do foretell!
As with a stern judicial air,

And with ample forehead bare
He enunciates the propositions broad.
Every ruling that he makes,
Each position that he takes,
Is a fraud.
And the jury, ah, the jury,
With their foreman, Uncle Drury,
In a fog,
While Judge Peter, sweet and smirking
With enunciation slow,
While his chair he keeps a-jerking
Says the law is so and so.

Oh, Judge Peter, learned Peter!
Mark the fierce discordant meter
Of his jaw!
See how Blackstone goes a whirling;
Poor old Kent is sent a curling;
"Here's your law!"
For Judge Peter saith so,
And he swingeth to and fro
And more important grows,
And his shining visage glows
While sweat trickles down his nose,
And he shuffles with his toes,
And he swings, swings, swings,
While loud his clapper rings
As he goes,
Belching law, law, law,
With a stern sonorous jaw,
As understood by Bell,
Peter Bell!

Laying down, down, down,
With a grave judicial frown,
The principles of law,
Of law, law, law,
Of a sort you never saw,
Waxing loud, loud, loud,
With his yell, yell, yell,

With a pompous air and proud
Proceeds his honor Peter Bell.
Oh, the Bell, Bell, Bell,
Oh the Woodson County Bell;
Oh the Bell, Bell, Bell, Bell,
Bell, Bell, Bell.

To the devil and his angels with thee, BELL!

"Old Fort" Leaves Kansas

An exploration in the Register of Deeds Office in the Neosho County Courthouse shows that several times J.N. Roach and his son Addison had sold, bought, resold, and bought again at least a portion of the lands they had claimed in Ladore Township. The implication, as stated by Betsy Warner of the Craig County Genealogical Society in her columns in *The Grand Laker* newspaper, was that the Roach family would fall on hard times and sell a portion of their lands for funds; then repurchase the land when their monetary fortunes were better. By 1877, as told by Ms. Warner, their lands were in foreclosure due to falling property values and some refinancing schemes J.N. Roach had undertaken to try to maintain possession. At this point the Roach family moved into the Indian Territory, locating in Craig County near the present town of Vinita.

From this point on the Roaches disappear from the narrative of Ladore. Ladore itself as a town was effectively lost to the pages of history and the streets of Parsons, Kansas where its buildings and people had largely been moved. There are two accounts found in the newspaper record that mention Addison being present in Parsons and the old connection with Ladore in the early 1900's, after James had died in 1895. These articles will serve as a bit of an epilog to the story of the Roach family in southeast Kansas.

The first article was published in the Parsons *Sun* in October of 1901 that covered the annual meeting of the Anti-Horse Thief Association (A.H.T.A.) that was held in Parsons that year. It is particularly ironic in that one of the suspicions that led to Addison's arrest in 1873 was that of horse theft. The passage in the article concerning Addison Roach is as follows:

--"Among the delegates who were in Parsons yesterday was Ad Roach, who now resides at Vinita, I.T. Roach was one of the first settlers in this vicinity and was living at Ladore before the railroad was built at Parsons, and when it was thought that if there was a large town in this section, Ladore would be that town. Roach knew all the old settlers in the northern part of Labette County and the southern part of Neosho County and has many friends among the old settlers who were pleased to see him yesterday."

- Parsons *Sun*, October 19, 1901, "The A.H.T.A. Annual Meeting"

The final mention so far found that deals with either James or Addison during the time that either was still alive was published in the Parsons *Sun* in June 1907, again briefly mentioning a visit by Addison to the town of Parsons.

--"A.A. Roach of Vinita was in the city today. He claims to be the oldest settler in this part of Kansas. It was his father for whom Fort Roach, now Ladore, was named. Twenty nine years ago he moved away from Parsons, and he had been an old settler here at that time. Southeastern Kansas is really old, after all, when one hears of these facts."

- Parsons *Sun*, June 17, 1907

Many further articles covering the community around the old town site of Ladore were published in the Neosho County and Labette County newspapers during the following years. Principally in the Parsons *Sun* or the Chanute *Tribune*, there would be weekly columns that would mention the local comings and goings and doings of the families of Ladore Township. The school was still in use well into the 20th century, as well as the church. There was an active, but small, local community of families who still occupied the lands of and around the town site as farmland.

The town of Ladore reached its height and then fell all in the year 1870. This is not atypical of many towns in the western United States during the latter half of the 19th century. As the railroad companies were formed and began the job of connecting the country with an intra-continental railroad system, towns would often be formed by groups of citizens speculating that their town would either be naturally placed along the line of a new railroad under construction or under the assumption that, if the town was sufficiently developed and sufficiently close to where a railroad might be planned, the railroad company could be induced to connect a spur or change its course to go through the town. If the town failed to win the railroad lottery, it would either be abandoned or moved to where the railroad was actually located. Other towns would form as planned stations or "end of the track" towns along the line of the road, then either thrive or die depending upon factors often not under their control.

In some ways Ladore experienced all of these roles. The Fort Scott *Monitor* had speculated in a story previously mentioned that one of Judge Roach's motivations for moving to Neosho County was to put himself and found a town along the proposed line of what became the M.K.&T. If such was the case, in that aim at least he was successful. As the M.K.&T. built down towards Ladore, the local citizens who had been building up a town for the better part of two years had inflicted upon them all the vices and flaws that accompanied an "end of the track" town as the ne'er-do-wells, the gamblers, hucksters, thieves and other dregs of society that would follow the railroad construction crews and cater to their desires for drink and entertainments managed to overwhelm the community for a time until that fateful night in May, 1870. Before, during and after the events of that May, the leaders of Ladore tried as best as they were able to induce the M.K.&T. to establish their shops and roundhouse facilities at Ladore. The preponderance of evidence points more towards that scenario than otherwise. When the die was cast by the M.K.&T. and Parsons established in October, Ladore played its final role as literally a town on the move.

Parsons drew people and buildings from several towns around the area who had, each in their way, played the railroad lottery; establishing themselves in the hope that they would become the place chosen by the M.K.&T. as it built its way through the Osage Ceded Lands. Montana and Labette City also lost buildings to Parsons, though small communities still exist at those places today. Dayton Station, Mendota and Ladore all are places that exist now largely only in name, induced to move and try their luck in the self-proclaimed "Infant Wonder."

So, how did the whiskey go down at Ladore? For a time, according to published accounts of citizens of the better class who were there, apparently the town had become as wild a town as the legends of southeast Kansas proclaim. However, Ladore was more than that. For a time it had ascended to an important political center in the region. It gave birth to the organization, the Settlers' Protective Association, that challenged the idea of railroad monopoly and the concept of excessive railroad land grants and managed to win, but at great cost. It had helped to develop some truly remarkable citizens, and from the kernel of what was best in Ladore sprung forth the fruit that helped to successfully establish the town of Parsons as the centerpiece of the M.K.&T. railroad for decades.

So,

Till uncovered and discovered and recovered,
And researched and unearthed and remembered,
And looked at to see how configured,
And documented, and recalled the legend,
And uncovered the story of its true end,
The people remember once more,
And add back to history's ledger the name of Ladore.

Bibliography

Books
B1. Case, Nelson, *History of Labette County, Kansas, and Representative Citizens*, Chicago Biographical Publishing Co., Chicago, IL, 1901.

B2. Connelley, William E., ***A Standard History of Kansas and Kansans***, Lewis Publishing Company, Chicago, IL, 1918.

B3. Cutler, William G., *History of the State of Kansas*, A. T. Andreas, Chicago, IL, 1883.

B4. Graves, W.W., *History of Neosho County*, Osage Mission Historical Society, St. Paul, KS, 1988.

B5. Curry, Mrs. Belle, *History of Parsons Kansas 1869-1895*, Parsons, KS, Bell Bookcraft Shop.

B6. Kansas State Board of Agriculture, *First Biennial Report of the State Board of Agriculture to the Legislature of the State of Kansas, for the Years 1877-8*, Rand, McNally & Co., Printers and Engravers, Chicago, IL, 1878.

B7. Masterson, V.V., *The Katy Railroad and the Last Frontier*, University of Missouri Press, Columbia, MO, 1978.

B8. Goodlander, C.W., *Memoirs and Recollections of C.W. Goodlander*, Ft. Scott Monitor Press, Ft. Scott, KS, 1900.

B9. HAR Co., "Historic Atlas of Kansas Counties CD-Rom", Original Atlas: "*The Official State Atlas of Kansas: Compiled from Government Surveys, County Records and Personal Investigations*", L.H. Everts & Co., 1887 (HAR, 2006).

B10. Duncan, L. Wallace, "*History of Neosho and Wilson Counties, Kansas*", Monitor Printing Co., Ft. Scott, KS, 1902

Newspapers
N1. The Parsons *Sun* – Parsons, KS

N2.   The New Chicago *Transcript* – Chanute, KS

N3.   The Neosho Valley (Iola) *Register* – Iola, KS

N4.   The Oswego *Register* – Oswego, KS

N5.   The Osage Mission *Transcript* – St. Paul, KS

N6.   The Parsons *Daily Republican* – Parsons, KS

N7.   The Southern Kansas (Chetopa) *Advance* – Chetopa, KS

N8.   The Osage Mission *Journal* – St. Paul, KS

N9.   The Neosho County *Journal* – St. Paul, KS

N10.   The Chanute *Tribune* – Chanute, KS

N11.   The Chanute *Times* – Chanute, KS

N12.   The Kansas City *Times* – Kansas City, MO

N13.   The Tioga *Herald* – Chanute, KS

N14.   The Fort Scott *Monitor* – Fort Scott, KS

N15.   The Thayer *Head Light* – Thayer, KS

N16.   The Logansport (IN) *Democratic Pharos* – Logansport, IN

N17.   The Logansport (IN) *Journal* – Logansport, IN

N18.   The Lawrence *Western Home Journal* – Lawrence, KS

N19.   The Lawrence *Daily Republican Journal* – Lawrence, KS

N20.   The Neosho County *Dispatch* – Erie, KS

N21.   The Independence *Republican* – Independence, KS

N22.   The (Lawrence) Kansas *Daily Tribune* – Lawrence, KS

N23.   The Parsons *Herald* – Parsons, KS

N24.   The Parsons *Eclipse* – Parsons, KS

N25.   The *Grand Laker* (affiliated with The Vinita *Daily Journal)* – Vinita, OK

N26.   The Topeka *Mail & Breeze* – Topeka, KS

N27.   Kansas Historical Society Microfilm Archives – Topeka, KS

Websites

W1.   **Indian Affairs: Laws and Treaties, Oklahoma State University, July 15, 1870 – 16 Stat. 362, (compiled 1929 by Charles Kappler, Government Printing Office), 2014;**
        http://digital.library.okstate.edu/kappler/Vol4/html_f iles/v4p0945c.html#mn5

W2.   **Indian Affairs: Laws and Treaties, Oklahoma State**

University, Compiled by Charles Kappler, Government Printing Office – Index, 2014; http://digital.library.okstate.edu/kappler/index.htm

W3. **Indian Affairs: Laws and Treaties, Compiled by Charles Kappler, Government Printing Office, Osage Treaties, Oklahoma State University – Index, 2014;** http://digital.library.okstate.edu/kappler/Vol2/toc.htm

W4. **The Pre-emption Act of 1841 – 5 Stat. 453:** http://www.infoplease.com/ce6/history/A0840041.html **Copy of Statute – Minnesota Legal History Project, 2014** http://www.minnesotalegalhistoryproject.org/assets/Microsoft%20Word%20-%20Preemption%20Act%20of%201841.pdf

W5. **The Homestead Act of 1862:** http://www.infoplease.com/ce6/history/A0824053.html **Transcript of Statute – Our Documents.Gov, 2014 http://www.ourdocuments.gov/doc.php?flash=true&doc=31&page=transcript**

W6. **Google Maps-Parsons, KS-Ladore Town Site-Lyon & Meadee Roads, 20th & 30th Roads, 2014:** www.maps.google.com

W7. **Kansas State Board of Agriculture First Biennial Report of 1878: Map of Neosho County:** http://skyways.lib.ks.us/genweb/archives/1878/neosho.shtml

W8. **Kansas State Board of Agriculture First Biennial Report of 1878: Map of Labette County:** http://skyways.lib.ks.us/genweb/archives/1878/allen.shtml

W9. **Canville Treaty (Osage Treaty of 1865) – 14 Stat. 687:** http://digital.library.okstate.edu/kappler/Vol2/treaties/osa0878.htm

W10.	**Osage Treaty of 1825 – 7 Stat. 240:**
	http://digital.library.okstate.edu/kappler/Vol2/treaties/osa0217.htm
W11.	**Ancestry.Com – Census and Marriage Records:**
	www.ancestry.com
W12.	**FindAGrave.Com – Grave Search:**
	www.findagrave.com
W13.	**Kansas Memory-County Map of Kansas, 2014:**
	www.kansasmemory.org
W14.	**Newspapers.**com
	http://www.newspapers.com/welcome/?odt=OofWaqWH7PSdnX9SoT9MgA==
W15.	**Newspaperarchive.com**
	http://newspaperarchive.com/ppclanding/welcomepagev3/

Libraries and Museums

L1.	Vinita, Oklahoma Public Library and Genealogy Room
L2.	Oswego Historical Society Museum
L3.	Parsons Public Library & Genealogy Room
L4.	Parsons Historical Society and Iron Horse Museum
L5.	Neosho County Historical Society Museum at St. Paul, Kansas
L6.	Fort Scott Genealogy Center
L7.	Erie Public Library
L8.	Erie Historical Society Museum
L9.	McCune Public Library and History Center
L10.	Chanute Public Library and History Room
L11.	Girard Public Library Genealogy Room
L12.	Kansas Historical Society Research Center
L13.	Independence Public Library

Return to Table of Contents

Picture Credits and References

I.   Ladore Cemetery – Neosho County, KS – Picture by David S. Beach, 2012

II.   James N. Roach Gravestone – Vinita, OK – Picture by David S. Beach, 2012

III.   Ladore Plat Map – Office of Register of Deeds – Neosho County, KS –
        Reconstructed by David S. Beach, 2012

IV.   Present Day Ladore – Source Image from Google Maps – Constructed by
        David S. Beach, 2012

V.   Ladore Lynching Woodcut – Found in *"The Katy Railroad and the Last Frontier"*
        by V.V. Masterson, 1978 and the Parsons *Sun* – Centennial Anniversary Edition, 1971

VI.   Versions of the Ladore Lynching Tables 1-4, by David S. Beach, 2014

VII.   Treaty of 1825 – The Osage Reservation base map, agriculture.ks.org, 2014, Constructed by David S. Beach, 2014

VIII.   Surveyor General for Kansas – Section 12, 10 Stat 308, July 22, 1854

IX.   Kansas Land Grant Act of 1863 – Image constructed by David S. Beach, 2014

X.   Neosho County Map – 1887, base map from Official Atlas of Kansas, land grant region constructed by David Beach, 2014

XI.   Labette County Map – 1887, base map from Official Atlas of Kansas, land grant region constructed by David Beach, 2014

Return to Table of Contents